A SKEPTIC'S GUIDE
TO THE TWELVE STEPS

Hazelden Titles of Related Interest

The Twelve Steps of Alcoholics Anonymous, Hazelden

Twelve Steps for Overeaters: An Interpretation of the Twelve Steps of Overeaters Anonymous, Elizabeth L.

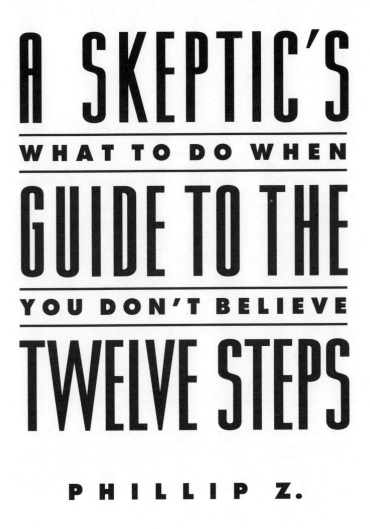

A SKEPTIC'S

WHAT TO DO WHEN

GUIDE TO THE

YOU DON'T BELIEVE

TWELVE STEPS

PHILLIP Z.

A Hazelden Book
HarperCollins*Publishers*

FIRST HARPERCOLLINS EDITION PUBLISHED IN 1991.

Library of Congress Cataloging-in-Publication Data

Z., Phillip.
   A skeptic's guide to the twelve steps : what to do when you don't believe / Philip Z. — 1st HarperCollins ed.
     p. cm.
   "A Hazelden book."
   Reprint. Originally published: Center City, Minn. : Hazelden Foundation, 1990.
   Includes bibliographical references and index.
   ISBN 0-06-255341-0
   1. Twelve-step programs—Religious aspects. I. Title.
BJ1596.Z25 1991
362.29'186—dc20   90-55843
                                        CIP

---

91 92 93 94 95 M-V 10 9 8 7 6 5 4 3 2 1

This edition is printed on acid-free paper that meets the American National Standards Institute Z39.48 Standard.

Contents

Preface

During the years I have been involved in Overeaters Anonymous, I have witnessed a dramatic increase in public awareness regarding addiction and its disastrous effect on the lives of addicts and those living and working with them. Bookstores all across America are devoting more and more shelf space to addiction and recovery materials. Articles reporting on new developments in the recovery field appear regularly in the press. Seemingly every day another public figure gives a testimonial in support of a Twelve Step program that changed his or her life. Just the other night, I watched a sketch on the popular television show, "Saturday Night Live," poking fun at Twelve Step programs and celebrities who sing the praises of recovery.

So, why another book when so much is already available on every aspect of addiction and recovery? How much more can be said about the nature of the addictive process, the Twelve Steps, or the effectiveness of Alcoholics Anonymous or any of the other Twelve Step programs? What could another book offer that has not already been said a hundred times before? And who am I to think that what I have to say has value beyond the experience, strength, and hope I can share at an Overeaters Anonymous meeting?

I have wrestled with these questions for the past two years. Before that, I had no intention of writing a book for publication. I kept a daily journal, in which I recorded the outer events and my inner reflections on my recovery process. I wrote down significant themes and images appearing in my meditations and dreams, and recorded my ongoing efforts to develop a meaningful understanding of a Higher Power. I also kept a section for significant quotes, along with my reflections on them, from books and tapes. I noticed that comments I was including in this section invariably touched on one or more of the Twelve Steps. Whether I was quoting a psychologist, a mystic, or a piece of program literature, I noted with each entry the Step or Steps to which it might best relate.

Eventually, I began sharing material from my journal with other people in and out of Overeaters Anonymous. I also began giving workshops to mental health professionals interested in the Twelve Steps, explaining how psychotherapy and the Twelve Step recovery process could be integrated, thereby enhancing the effectiveness of both.

Those people who seemed most interested in what I had to say were often quite skeptical about the Twelve Step process and things they had heard about the programs. Concepts such as surrendering one's will and life to God were particularly unsettling to those who, like myself, respond to matters of religion and spirituality with skepticism. Hearing me share my understanding and experience proved helpful to many of them.

This book is intended for a wider audience than I have been able to reach in personal encounters. I hope it provides a way of approaching the Twelve Steps that encourages others to undertake the spiritual journey of recovery despite their skepticism. I also hope this book helps those who live and work with addicts, including the professionals who treat them, to better understand the spiritual nature of addiction and the necessity for a spiritual basis to any program of recovery.

I also questioned whether I should put my full name on the book. Many people outside the program have encouraged me to put my name on it; some of my friends and colleagues have been quite upset with me for choosing not to do so. However, those I trust in the program agreed that a book such as this, where I record my personal recovery experiences, should be published without revealing my identity to the general public.

For those unfamiliar with Twelve Step programs, let me explain. Alcoholics Anonymous and the other Twelve Step programs are guided by Twelve Traditions that serve as principles for their governance, to protect the fellowships from various forms of pressure and political turmoil that often destroy organizations. At the same time, these Traditions remind members that certain attitudes and behaviors, including the belief that one can publicly hold him- or herself out as an authority on recovery, can be harmful to the individual member.

Tradition Eleven reads, "Our public relations policy is based on attraction rather than promotion; we need always maintain personal anonymity at the level of press, radio and films."[1] Its language is clear and unambiguous. To identify oneself at the level of the media as a member of a specific Twelve Step program violates that Tradition.

Increasingly, this Tradition is being broken by well-intentioned individuals wishing to share their experiences and the miracle of their recovery. Each of us is free to violate this Tradition; no one is punished or banished from the program for his or her transgression. Even so, and despite a part of me that would love to see my name on the cover of a book that might sell widely and be of help to others, I have chosen to honor the tradition of anonymity.

Finally, I want to make clear that I am sharing my personal experience and orientation to the Twelve Steps and recovery. Each of us, in the last analysis, must find an orientation that feels right as we take our individual journey.

No author, sponsor, therapist, or Twelve Step program can provide anyone with all of the answers. They can only offer suggestions for tapping the strength, hope, and wisdom each of us must eventually find within.

Acknowledgments

First and foremost, I extend my heartfelt gratitude and express my deepest respect to the cofounders of Alcoholics Anonymous, Bill W. and Dr. Bob, for persevering on their journey of recovery and passing on their experience, strength, and hope.

I thank all my friends in Overeaters Anonymous for the help they've provided along the way, particularly my sponsors, Susan S., Otis H., and Bill B. They have given direction by exemplifying the Twelve Step way of life, which in the long run has been more helpful than any theory or suggestion they could have offered.

I especially thank my sister, Laura, who first suggested that I go to an OA meeting, thereby launching me on this adventure. I have been delighted to share my recovery experience with her.

I am also grateful to many friends and colleagues who encouraged me to write this book, particularly Dr. Terry Kupers, Kim Chernin, Elad Levinson, and Theo Gund for their continued support and valuable suggestions and criticisms.

I also offer my appreciation to Renate Stendahl for her expert editing and tender hand-holding in the early stages of this book, and to my editor at Hazelden for his support and enthusiasm in the later stages.

And finally, I thank and dedicate this book to Tobey Hiller, my wife and best friend. Our relationship together, both before and now in my recovery, is the other great gift I have been given.

The search may begin with restless feelings, as if one were being watched. One runs in all directions and sees nothing. Yet one senses that there is a source for the deep restlessness, and the path that leads there is not a path to a strange land but the path home. . . . The journey is hard, for the secret place where we have always been is overgrown with thorns and thickets of ideas, of fears and defenses, prejudices and depressions.

— *Peter Matthiesson*

If you fulfill the pattern that is peculiar to yourself you have loved yourself, you have accumulated, you have abundance; you bestow virtue then because you have lustre, you radiate, from your abundance something overflows. But if you hate yourself, if you have not accepted your pattern, then there are hungry animals, prowling cats and other beasts in your constitution which get at your neighbors like flies in order to satisfy the appetites which have failed to satisfy. Therefore, Nietzsche says to those people who have not fulfilled their individual pattern that the bestowing soul is lacking. There is no radiation, no real warmth: there is hunger and secret stealing.

— *Carl Jung*

Introduction

One morning in early 1985, just before my forty-second birthday, I stepped on my bathroom scale and looked at its little glass window with the red arrow. This was not an unusual way for me to begin the day; I had engaged in this daily ritual since my early teens. What was out of the ordinary was the fact that, for the past several months, I had stopped performing it. But on that particular morning I awoke, went into the bathroom, and stepped on the scale without reflection. Watching the black lines and numbers blur past the red arrow until they stopped one small black line before the number 200, I broke into a cold sweat. On my five-foot, seven-inch frame I had managed to reach 199 pounds.

The scale needs adjusting, I thought. Stepping onto the bathroom floor I watched the dial spin, nervously hoping my assumption would be confirmed. But when it came to rest, the arrow pointed directly at the number zero. *My God, how has this happened? I have gained at least twenty-five pounds during the last three or four months.* In truth, family and friends had been gracefully expressing concern regarding my physical condition for some time. Their comments had been met with irritation and stony denial.

I had been putting off buying new clothes for months, even though my size thirty-eight pants were stretching tightly around my spreading waist and thighs and my shirts spread open between the buttons whenever I sat down. When I did venture into a department store, the only clothes I could bear to try on were sweaters because they were bulky and tended to cover my body. I could not find the courage to try on pants because I didn't want to face the truth about how large a size I would need. What lengths I was going to in my attempt to hide the obvious from myself and the world! Somehow, I thought I could keep my obesity a secret.

In the days that followed, I ruminated over my condition and the possible causes for my inability to keep my weight under control. Literature from the field of eating disorders consistently attributed obesity to underlying depression and feelings of low self-esteem. I certainly did not fit the clinical picture. On the contrary, with the exception of my weight, I was quite happy and excited with the way my life was going. I had a pleasant and enriching family life, a thriving practice as a psychotherapist, and a community of good friends. Nevertheless, whatever emotional factors led to my condition the fact remained that I had become clinically obese, more than fifty pounds over the current medically recommended weight for my height.

I gave some thought to trying to diet but could muster little enthusiasm. Having tried and failed so many times over the years, I was certain dieting could not bring about permanent weight loss for me. I had begun buying diet books in high school. While not particularly overweight, I was nevertheless obsessed with my body image.

During my college days, I continued experimenting with the latest fad diets that were frequently featured in books and magazines at supermarket check-out counters. I would be lured by promises of quick weight loss and permanent thinness to be obtained without feelings of hunger or deprivation. Some diets espoused high amounts of animal protein and no carbohydrates. Other diets called for eating only from a narrow range of foods. For days I lived on nothing but grapefruit, spinach, and eggs. At other times, my diet consisted almost exclusively of beef, chicken, fish, and cooked greens. Along with millions of other men and women unhappy with their weight and body image, I was attracted to these bizarre eating regimes precisely because they were novel. They promised a quick and easy permanent solution to my weight problem.

In addition to fad diets, I periodically tried healthy, balanced eating plans—the rational approach to weight management. Some plans called for limiting caloric intake by one method or another. Other plans stressed combining exercise with low-calorie food consumption. While I felt more virtuous on these "healthy, balanced" diet programs than when following a fad diet, I found them no more effective in making and keeping me thin.

Throughout my twenties and thirties I continued the struggle. I had become a yo-yo dieter, gaining weight to a point I found unbearable, then dieting. During the diet, I would lose a substantial amount of weight, only to regain it later along with five or ten extra pounds.

In addition to dieting, I tried other approaches to weight maintenance. In my desperate search for the secret of permanent thinness, I attended several workshops designed to establish a new consciousness regarding food and destructive eating habits. On one occasion, I sat in a large group of overweight people, smelling and fondling different foods and finally holding them in my mouth for long periods of time until they became paste. We were supposedly learning to discriminate which foods we ate for nutrition and which we ate to merely satisfy taste cravings. This knowledge was apparently going to help the participants eat only when hungry and only those foods that the body required for nutrition and physical well-being. The theory seemed sound and the workshop was interesting, but the experience brought no changes either in my ability to control my eating or in my weight.

At another workshop, I learned behavioral techniques for controlling food consumption. I was taught to eat my meals more slowly by putting down my fork between bites, eating only when seated, and chewing each forkful of food a certain number of times before swallowing. These workshops were fun. I met wonderful people. But the experiences did not solve my weight problem. I would use the techniques for a short while and then gradually forget to use them and within weeks return to my old eating habits.

I had personally undergone psychotherapy several times over the years, both to address personal issues and because of my work as a therapist. One issue I always worked on was my weight. The therapists I saw were excellent. Psychotherapy helped me a great deal with a number of issues apart from my weight. I was also able to gain insight and understanding into the underlying motivations for my weight problems, but no permanent changes came in that area. Sometimes I would have a breakthrough—some insight or emotional release would seem to result in a period of moderate eating, and I would be elated that I had finally changed my relationship with food. But after a period of rational eating and some weight loss, I would soon return to overeating. The pounds would increase, and, before long, all the weight I had worked so hard to take off would return, plus additional pounds.

Another approach that seemed promising was physical exercise. Instead of diet books, now I read books about running and other forms of aerobic exercise. I learned all about target pulse rates and joined the jogging craze. For several years, I thought I had found the answer. I could eat all I wanted and still keep my weight under control by running six to ten miles a day. I looked and felt terrific. Unfortunately, after a while all the pounding began to affect my joints, and I began experiencing pain in my knees and lower back. Eventually, I had to retire my running shoes and I quickly gained back the weight.

With years of effort and failure behind me, I had little enthusiasm for undertaking another diet. But fear and shame are powerful motivators, and so I began my search for another dietary approach to my problem. At the time, I had no way to know that this was going to be my last attempt at controlling my weight by limiting food consumption.

A few weeks after my shocking discovery that I had reached 199 pounds, I ran into a friend whom I had not seen for several months. I noticed that she had lost a significant amount of weight since our last meeting and expressed curiosity about how she had done it. With a great deal of enthusiasm, she explained that she had been going to a relatively new, nationally franchised diet program, where she had lost weight quickly and easily. She said she had been maintaining her weight loss for several months, adding that the company prided itself on follow-up studies indicating that a very high percentage of its successful dieters had maintained their weight losses for over one year. I was impressed, as I had never been able to maintain my goal weight for more than a few weeks. I knew that there were statistics indicating that 98 percent of all people who go on *any* diet plan or program will regain the weight they lose within two years. What my friend had told me gave me hope that by going to this program, I might beat those discouraging odds.

I signed up for the diet program, paid my money, and began following the eating plan I was given. I ate only what was allowed on my plan in the quantities prescribed. I took the food-supplement pills my diet counselor gave me each day when I came for my weigh-in and pep talk. I bought and ate the various food products my diet counselor sold. My faithful adherence to the plan brought results. As weeks passed, I lost weight quickly and easily, just as advertised. But as my counselor and I took pleasure in my weight losses, I kept telling her I was anxious about what would happen once I reached my goal weight. What would I do when I no longer came in daily and followed a strict diet? Was I going to have to eat skinned chicken breasts and rye crackers for the rest of my life?

She told me not to worry, the program would provide me with a maintenance diet and the support of the company and its staff would continue to be available. She assured me I was developing permanent eating habits that would allow me to maintain my weight loss while following a flexible maintenance diet.

I began having the disturbing thought that this nice diet lady did not really understand what I was up against. Everything she said sounded reasonable. Nevertheless, even as the weeks of success grew into months, I continued worrying that something inside of me would propel me back to over-eating. I did not know what this "something" was, but I knew that it was sleeping quietly in a dark corner of my mind even as my family, friends, and I delighted in my improved physical and emotional state.

When I reached my goal weight I had lost almost fifty pounds. I looked and felt like a new person. I bought new clothes in the same sizes I had worn in high school. At this point, my diet counselor put me on a maintenance eating plan. In addition to following the expanded diet I was to come in to be weighed several times a week. At first I followed the new diet, weighed in regularly, and kept my weight stable. Then I began having occasional slips, little bouts of cheating. One night I made a midnight attack on ice cream. A few days later, I indulged in a large buffet lunch at a Chinese restaurant near my office, rather than eat the lunch I had packed in the morning. Walking toward the restaurant, I told myself that this time I would eat only one plateful of food. But once I began eating, as always in the past, I ended up going back for seconds and thirds.

I also began bingeing on peanuts again, despite not having touched them during the months I was going to the diet program. Stopping off at a market on the way home, I would tell myself it would be okay to buy a small bag of peanuts. I could eat a few and put the rest away in the kitchen cupboard. When I returned to my car, however, I had the large, economy-size bag of peanuts clutched in my hands. Driving home, I would steer the car with one hand while shelling and eating peanuts with the other. By the time I reached my house, peanut shells would be scattered over my lap, the driver's seat, and the car floor. I would feel bloated and sick to my stomach.

I could not explain to myself why I was engaging in the self-destructive eating behaviors that I had avoided during the many months I was following a strict diet plan. Out of shame,

I did not want to tell my diet counselor about my slips; I wanted to keep my failings secret. Each time I went in to be weighed, I would wear lighter clothes, hoping to hide the weight I knew I was gaining *until I could get things back under control.* Each morning, I would rededicate myself to follow the diet, but I was unable to accomplish what had been so easy at the beginning.

My weight continued to increase as the old eating behaviors became more frequent. I felt terrified and confused. I had hoped this time I would be able to keep the weight off. But that deep sense of dread and hopelessness that I had tried to put out of my mind throughout the months of successful dieting was proving to be an accurate prognostication. My loss of control with food became greater as I gained thirty-five pounds in less than two months. I stopped going to the diet program and did not return the messages my counselor left on my answering machine. I had failed again. I knew it was only a matter of time before I would regain all the weight I had lost and begin to hit new weight highs.

On the first Sunday in February 1986, after a family brunch, my sister took me aside to explain that she had been going to meetings of Overeaters Anonymous for about a month and was very excited about her experiences. Both of us had struggled with our weight problems for years. Like me, she had tried just about everything to find the key to permanent thinness. She handed me a few pamphlets. Between the moment she mentioned Overeaters Anonymous and when I began reading the first pamphlet, visions floated in my head: revival meetings, religious brainwashings, and disheveled alcoholics standing around dark, dingy church basements speaking with slurred speech. Surely my sister had lost her mind. I pictured her along with other fat men and women on their knees, praying to God to make them thin.

Nothing on earth could induce me to go to any meeting offered by an organization that evoked such disturbing images.

In the first pamphlet, the nature of compulsive overeating was described with the explanation that this condition was physical, emotional, and spiritual. Listed were a number of yes-or-no questions, which I began to answer. Did I often eat in secret? Did I eat until my stomach hurt or until I felt sick? Did I regularly eat when I was not hungry? Did I devote excessive amounts of time to thoughts about buying food, cooking, eating food, and dieting? One after another I was compelled to answer in the affirmative.

In the next pamphlet, the idea was suggested that compulsive overeaters had an unusual relationship with food, much like alcoholics and other addicts' relationships with alcohol or other drugs. Neither dieting nor behavioral change alone could stop such people from overeating any more than alcoholics could control their consumption or stop drinking permanently through exercise of willpower. What was needed, according to the pamphlet, were physical, emotional, and spiritual changes in the compulsive overeater. I was not clear what such changes might involve, but the connection between alcoholism and compulsive overeating made immediate sense to me. My sister was pleased when I told her I was willing to go to at least one meeting to learn more about Overeaters Anonymous.

The following Wednesday evening in a church basement near my home I attended my first OA meeting. What I learned and experienced at that meeting and at hundreds I have attended since that night has dramatically changed my life. I came with a minimum of curiosity and a thin thread of hope. I also brought a great deal of suspicion and skepticism. Had a book like this been available, it might have eased my doubts and given me an understanding of the process I was about to undergo.

Many books are being written these days praising the power of Twelve Step programs. Their authors extoll the importance of the recovery process in helping those suffering from various addictive and compulsive illnesses. Other books are critical of various aspects of this growing movement. Some take exception to the concept of alcoholism as a disease or criticize the programs for suggesting that abstinence is the only solution to the problem of substance abuse. There is concern that *all* emotional difficulties are being reduced to problems of addiction by apostles of the Twelve Steps.

My professional colleagues in the mental health field have mixed responses to seeing more and more people coming into therapy who are also working the Twelve Steps and going to meetings. Most traditionally trained psychotherapists are unclear about how to integrate psychotherapy and participation in a recovery program. Many have difficulty adapting their theories and techniques to the demands of providing therapy to clients who are also engaged in the recovery process. Having little or no firsthand knowledge or experience with these programs, they are naturally often critical of things they hear, particularly from their clients. For example, one of the primary goals of psychotherapy is helping clients become more independent and self-reliant. Thus, therapists are likely to be distressed to hear a client talk about accepting personal powerlessness and surrendering his or her will and life to God and the program.

I hope to strike a balance between the view that Twelve Step programs are the answer to all emotional problems on the one hand, and the attitude that these programs are nothing more than antirational, self-help cults on the other. While I have witnessed the tremendous healing power of Twelve Step programs, as this book will show, some aspects still disturb me. Despite my concerns, however, I am convinced by my experience and the experiences of many others that adherence to the Twelve Steps and participation in fellowships of recovering persons can bring about extraordinary physical, emotional, and spiritual healing.

* * *

I once heard someone say in an OA meeting that the Twelve Step programs are more difficult for intelligent, inquiring people. He said he felt blessed not to have that problem. He was expressing a view I have often heard in meetings, that success comes only through following the suggestions of those with more experience in the program. I am always disturbed by such views, having always valued and depended on my ability and willingness to think independently and to question and investigate new ideas. My recovery has come through maintaining a skeptical, but inquiring mind. I have not found it necessary to suspend my capacity to think critically—to question the ideas and opinions of others—in order to grow emotionally and spiritually. Quite the contrary. I have found that, for me, Twelve Step recovery demands rigorous thinking, honest self-appraisal, and commitment to changing deep and compelling habits of mind and action. The Twelve Steps are hardly pacifiers serving to simply relieve us from having to confront the inevitable challenges life presents. The journey from compulsion to compassion requires one's constant willingness to accept reality and avoid reliance on the kinds of superficial, magical beliefs that only appear to relieve one of responsibility for his or her life.

A person who is beginning to sense the suffering of life is, at the same time, beginning to awaken to deeper realities, truer realities. For suffering smashes to pieces the complacency of our normal fictions about reality, and forces us to become alive in a special sense—to see carefully, to feel deeply, to touch ourselves and our worlds in ways we have heretofore avoided. It has been said, and I truly think that suffering is the first grace. In a special sense, suffering is almost a time of rejoicing, for it marks the birth of creative insight.

— *Ken Wilber*

The moment we accept the place where we may seem helpless, it can cease to be the deepest truth about us. . . . The process is painstaking, and for it to proceed we need great compassion for ourselves—exactly the way we are. And we allow the Universe to be exactly the way it is. Through this process we find that we are no longer pitting ourselves against things. We're opening to life—first by opening ourselves, and then gradually expanding outward.

— *Ram Dass*

An addiction exists when a person's attachment to a sensation, an object, or another person is such as to lessen his appreciation of an ability to deal with other things in his environment, or in himself, so that he has become increasingly dependent on that experience as his only source of gratification. A person will be predisposed to addiction to the extent that he cannot establish a meaningful relationship to his environment as a whole, and thus cannot develop a fully elaborated life.
— *Stanton Peele from* The Making of Addiction

CHAPTER ONE

Admitting Powerlessness

We admitted we were powerless over food — that our lives had become unmanageable. *

Entering my house after a day of seeing clients, I call out to my wife. The silence informs me that she has not yet come home. Walking into the kitchen, I consider what to make for dinner. I think back to what I had for lunch. What was it? Oh, yes.

Having eaten a lot over the weekend, I woke up determined to eat lightly for a few days. I packed some low-fat cottage cheese and fruit for lunch and took it to the office. However, by 10:00 in the morning I felt very hungry. So, after a short inner battle, I ate the cottage cheese and fruit during a break between two therapy sessions.

A sense of shame comes over me as I recall going out at 12:30 and having a large ham and cheese sandwich on a french roll with a bag of potato chips. I remember being quite full after that meal, but nevertheless by 3:00 in the afternoon I was ravenous again. My shame grows as I recall that, be-

---

* Step One, the Twelve Steps of Overeaters Anonymous, adapted from the Twelve Steps of Alcoholics Anonymous. The complete Twelve Steps of AA appear on page 221.

tween sessions, I slipped out to a nearby store for a large bag of corn chips, which I promptly devoured.

Reflecting on my food consumption for the day, I resolve to eat a low-calorie dinner. As I open the refrigerator and remove a package of defrosted hamburger, my eye catches a bowl of tuna and mayonnaise on the upper shelf. As though I hadn't noticed the tuna, I close the door and take the hamburger over to the counter. But as I begin removing the wrapper and putting the meat in a bowl, my thoughts float back to that bowl of tuna fish. *My wife must have made tuna for her luncheon sandwich,* I think to myself. *I really love tuna. It would have been great to have had a tuna sandwich for lunch.* Suddenly, it seems important that my wife never adds onion when she makes tuna salad and this thought arouses a momentary flash of anger toward her. How the hell can she make tuna salad without onion?

I return to the refrigerator for some onion I intend to chop and add to the hamburger. As I remove the onion, I take out the bowl of tuna at the same time. A desperate but quiet voice arises in my head suggesting that it is not a good idea to start eating the tuna so close to dinner. But I'm now looking in the cupboard for those crackers that go so well with tuna. Great, there are still some in the box. I take down the box and cut up the onion. Some of the chopped onion goes into the bowl with the hamburger and the rest goes into the tuna.

I am suddenly overcome with anxiety. What if someone comes home and catches me eating? In my momentary panic, I quickly grab a few crackers, dip them into the tuna two and three at a time, and stuff them into my mouth. As I begin reaching for the next handful of crackers, I pass into a familiar state of altered consciousness. I can see my hand, the box of crackers, the bowl of hamburger, but I am not sure what has become of the person I believe myself to be. The father, husband, successful psychotherapist in his early forties is gone, replaced by a large void without feelings, without sense of self, devouring food. I am like the hungry ghosts described in Buddhist mythology as having huge empty stomachs and tiny mouths. So small are their mouths and so enormous their bellies that they cannot consume food quickly enough to ease their formidable hunger.

The crackers are gone. Looking down into the bowl that only moments ago was filled with tuna, onion, and mayonnaise, I see only small pieces of tuna and a few smears of mayonnaise. I wipe the bowl with my finger and quickly put my finger in my mouth, licking off every morsel of food. I am flooded with familiar feelings of shame and remorse. *My God, why did I eat all of that stuff just before dinner?* I ask myself, knowing I have absolutely no answer. Almost at once, I am relieved of all discomfort by the memory of some cheese I had noticed in the refrigerator when removing the bowl of tuna fish. So what if all the crackers are gone? I can put some mustard (low calorie) on a few slices of cheese. Removing the cheese and mustard, I also grab the jar of mayonnaise and bring all my treasures to the counter.

Before consuming the current objects of my desire, I throw the hamburger into a pan and put water on to boil for noodles and frozen peas. Having taken care of the family dinner, I return to my snack. I cut, prepare with mustard and mayonnaise, and devour slice after slice of the cheese. I am beginning to feel sick. I think I should stop eating, but as there is only a little cheese left, I finish it off.

As the hamburger is ready to turn, my wife comes home. She walks into the kitchen and asks how things are going. "Fine," I say. She looks at me for a moment. We both know I'm lying. The expression on her face reveals her pain and sense of helplessness. In this moment of awkwardness, neither of us speaks. Finally, I relieve the tension, announcing dinner will be ready in a few minutes. My wife sets the table. I bring the food into the dining room and we sit down to eat dinner together. A heavy silence fills the air.

Scenes like this had been a regular occurrence for years. In the period shortly before I went to my first Overeaters

Anonymous meeting, they happened, in one form or another, every day. I was terrified that these eating patterns had become permanent. They were driving my weight higher and higher.

It was tremendous fear and only a thin ray of hope that motivated me to go to my first Overeaters Anonymous meeting. Many failed attempts to deal with my weight problem in the past precluded any optimism. Recognizing myself in the description of the compulsive overeater presented in the pamphlet my sister had shown me, I went to the meeting willing to learn more about what this program had to say about compulsive overeating. But my curiosity was sandwiched between powerful feelings of hopelessness, suspicion, and fear. What most frightened me about going to the meeting was the fact that, by showing up, I was admitting publicly that I had a serious problem I could not solve alone.

That the meeting was in the basement of a church immediately made me uncomfortable. I had been raised in a Jewish home, but had not entered any place of worship since adolescence. I had no interest in anything religious and most certainly did not want to spend time in a church. Nevertheless, my curiosity and desperation motivated me to go in.

The room was fairly large. About forty chairs had been set in rows. I immediately took one of the aisle chairs in the back of the room, strategically placing my jacket on the chair next to me. A man, starting a pot of coffee and arranging tea bags and Styrofoam cups on a table at the side of the room, turned to me and said hello. I returned his greeting, smiling nervously.

Then a woman entered the room carrying folders and a big binder. Thinking she must be in charge, I went to her and asked if she was the person who collected the fees. She smiled, took my hand, and told me that OA did not charge any fee. She explained that people who regularly attended meetings were asked to make contributions to cover rent and expenses, but that newcomers were not asked to contribute.

She suggested I attend several meetings before deciding if OA was for me. She added that if I wished, I could use my money to purchase program literature that would explain Overeaters Anonymous and provide a basis on which I could decide if the program was right for me.

I was aware of feeling extremely vulnerable as she took my hand. Her explanation that Overeaters Anonymous did not charge any fees shocked me. Having been raised in a family where suspicion of strangers was a fundamental rule of life, I became wary at what appeared to be an offer of something for nothing.

My years of experience trying to lose weight had led to the reasonable conclusion that all methods of weight loss carried a price tag. Diet books can make millions of dollars for their authors; some weight-loss programs are so successful that they sell stock on Wall Street. Diet clinics and doctors often make fantastic sums of money prescribing the latest diet pills or "medical" remedies. The often fanatical drive of Americans, particularly women, to lose weight generates enormous profits. *Surely there is some gimmick to this organization,* I thought as I returned to my seat. Somewhat disoriented and very anxious, I watched people begin filling the room.

At exactly 8:00 P.M., the meeting began with a group prayer. I was uncomfortable. *These people don't waste a minute before pushing the God stuff,* I thought. Then people took turns reading aloud from printed handouts. I kept hearing the word, *God.* Each time I heard it, I cringed. *What the hell am I doing here?* I asked myself. *I don't believe in God; I hate groups of believers. In fact, I hate all groups.*

You don't have much of a choice, I'm afraid, was the answer I heard in my head. Looking around I saw about forty people, most of them women. I was relieved to see five or six men present, as most of the diet and weight programs I had tried were almost exclusively attended by women. I felt pleased, realizing that I would not be the only man attending OA meetings, were I to continue. Some of the men and women were very obese; some were, like myself, moderately over-weight. Many were quite slim. *Why,* I wondered, *did they come to this meeting?* If I had been slim, this was the last place I would have wanted to be—in some dingy church basement on a winter night, saying prayers and talking about bingeing, feelings, and God.

At a certain point, a woman who looked to be in her early thirties stood in front of the group and was introduced as the speaker for the evening. Slender and quite animated, she was dressed in bright colors and wore lots of beautiful rings and bracelets. By her presence, she demanded the attention of the group. I was not sure what I expected, but she was definitely not it.

When she began describing her life before coming into Overeaters Anonymous, she spoke about years of bingeing and secret eating. She told stories about stealing food from supermarkets and friends' cupboards. She laughed as she related her endless search for the magic diet that would bring permanent thinness. She explained that in OA she had come to understand that she had always used food to avoid feelings that seemed unbearable. She had come to realize and admit how secretive, controlling, and dishonest she had been in her relationships with others. Her frankness and honesty amazed me. I had never heard anyone acknowledge doing things I thought only I had done.

She went on to describe her early days in OA. Once again I was in for a surprise. She was quite explicit when relating her initial reaction to OA. She said, quite bluntly, that when she first came to the program she couldn't take "the God shit." She kept repeating the phrase throughout her talk. I was shocked every time I heard it. If that wasn't enough to challenge my assumptions about these "true believers," I noticed everyone else in the room roaring with laughter and nodding in agreement every time she repeated it. *What the hell was going on here? One minute these people were praying to*

God and the next they were laughing at a member's irreverent telling of her difficulty with God talk.

When the speaker finished, others in the room took turns talking. Each person began by saying his or her name and then declaring he or she was a compulsive overeater. Then the group greeted the person by saying, "Hi," and the person's name. I thought this ritual was quite silly and childish. I felt embarrassed each time it was repeated. On each occasion, I remained silent. No praying! No "Hi, so-and-so!" No nothing!

Some people spoke about their troubles with food and life situations, while others shared with excitement current successes in their lives. Most praised Overeaters Anonymous for changing their lives. Occasionally, someone said that he or she had lost weight and was maintaining abstinence from compulsive overeating only through God's grace. One man offered thanks to what he called his Higher Power for helping him stay away from a dessert served at a dinner party he had attended the night before.

I could handle the praise being given to the program. But I wanted to bolt from the room when I heard people attribute weight loss and the ability to resist food to God or some Higher Power. While I liked the main speaker and was encouraged to hear of people's successes in the program, I was put off by what seemed to me to be simplistic religious nonsense. Thoughts kept going through my head that OA was not for me. How could a person with my intelligence and sophistication come to meetings where people talked about being powerless over food and espoused their belief that God loved and took care of them? How could grown men and women state openly that, "because they believed in God, *He* was preventing them from eating certain foods"? As the meeting progressed, I began feeling more and more critical of these people and this program.

Then, over the roar of criticism and judgment filling my head, I heard someone say that she wanted to speak particularly to the newcomers. She looked right at me as she explained that most of the people in the room had been put off by much of what they heard at the first few meetings they had attended. She suggested that those of us who were new to Overeaters Anonymous come back to several more meetings before making up our minds about the program. She wanted us to know that each person in OA had his or her own way of understanding and working the program and that if we heard things that felt unacceptable to us, we could disregard them. "Take what you want and leave the rest," she said. She concluded by admitting that she had been pretty turned off when she first came to OA, but that she was glad she had remained. Her comments brought some relief. I told myself all that was important for now was that I shared my compulsive overeating problem with these people, many of whom no longer ate in destructive ways.

At the end of the meeting, everyone stood in a circle and joined hands. I silently held the hands of two other people as the group recited the Lord's Prayer. I could hardly contain my discomfort. When the prayer ended, everyone shouted, "Keep coming back. It works." The people began hugging each other and talking wildly in small groups. I couldn't get out of the room fast enough. Quickly grabbing my jacket, I shot out the door without speaking to a soul.

I sat quietly for a while in the refuge of my car. Then, suddenly, I started to cry. I cried for some time, sitting there in my parked car on a quiet side street in the darkness. I asked myself why I was crying and, in search of an answer, began reflecting on things I had heard and seen in the meeting. I thought about the warmth and joy I felt in the room. I remembered the laughter, but also the calm concern shown to people who had shared powerful feelings. These people had laughed and spoken openly about things I had kept hidden from the world for so long. And they could sit quietly when someone publicly expressed pain or sorrow or anger. No one seemed driven to try to fix anyone or offer suggestions and verbal reassurances.

I realized that my tears came from a sense of hope. I had been with people who shared my problem, a number of whom no longer lived in shame and defeat. In that moment, I could finally admit to myself that I was a compulsive over-eater, that I had a peculiar relationship to food not shared by everyone: I could no longer maintain the delusion that I could control my eating. Even as I faced the awful truth, I also felt hope in the realization that there were people in that meeting who had felt the same.

I could finally admit that, for years, I had been powerless to restrict or control my eating. In the face of overwhelming evidence, I had managed to delude myself that one day I would find the magic diet or technique. During the meeting, I was compelled to confront the reality that I would never be able to control my weight by dieting or behavioral tech-niques. I was relieved to realize that I suffered from a condi-tion that affected me physically, emotionally, and spiritually. I did not overeat because I had no willpower nor because I was too much of a pig to stay on a diet. While I was com-forted by this discovery, I was still unhappy that the solution seemed to require praying to God. The idea seemed ludicrous.

After sitting in my car for about twenty minutes, I started for home. As I drove, I continued to think about the meeting and my reactions to what I had experienced. My rational mind was dead set against returning, principally because of the God stuff. But some other part of me wanted to see and hear more. The more emotional side of me had been moved by what I had experienced: I had felt a sense of validation and common experience. I knew that, for an hour and a half, I had spent time with a community of people who knew the hell I had been going through for years. I wanted more contact with that community. So, despite my discomfort with the

God talk and the prayers, I resolved to go to meetings and take their suggestions, at least for a while.

During the weeks that followed, I attended meetings almost daily. Naturally, I wanted to know what the people there did to take the weight off and keep it off. So I spoke to several of them about what I should do about my food intake. Some suggested cutting sugar and white flour out of my diet; others said I should eat three weighed-and-measured meals a day with nothing in between. Nearly everyone I spoke to said I had to be willing to make achieving and maintaining abstinence the top priority in my life. It was suggested that I find a *food sponsor*, a person who could show me more about how the program works and help me make a food plan. While a food plan seemed a great deal like a diet, I did what was suggested and asked a trim young woman who had been abstinent for several years to be my sponsor. She helped me develop my food plan and asked me to call her every morning to tell her what I was planning to eat throughout the day. She suggested calling her or someone else in the program whenever I felt like deviating from my plan. This was shaping up to be a lot like a diet club, but since I had decided to give OA a chance, I took my food sponsor's suggestions.

The food plan I developed was a modification of the diet I had been given at the diet program, where I had recently lost fifty pounds. It consisted of three weighed-and-measured meals daily with no caloric foods between. I made a list of foods I tended to overeat and committed to eliminating them from my diet. I listed nuts and nut products, cheese and other fatty foods, because I knew that whenever I started eating those foods I had a hard time stopping. I was told that I was *allergic* to those foods and needed to refrain from eating them lest I trigger the binge cycle. I accepted the explanation that for compulsive overeaters, certain foods are addictive, just as alcohol is for the alcoholic.

Breakfast consisted of a measured portion of cereal, milk, and a piece of fruit. As an alternative, I might choose a piece of whole-grain bread along with a half cup of low-fat cottage cheese and a piece of fruit. Lunch consisted of a salad with two cups of greens and other raw vegetables, a slice of whole-wheat bread, a four-ounce portion of chicken or fish, and a piece of fruit. Dinner was the same as lunch with the addition of a cup of cooked vegetables and with no fruit.

I began losing weight. The program, as I understood it, worked, and I was very excited and positive about OA. I followed my food plan day after day, faithfully calling my food sponsor and going to four or five meetings a week. Within two months I lost over twenty-five pounds: I was another OA miracle. Soon I was being asked to chair meetings so I could share my success story with others. I would travel to meetings in town and in neighboring cities, describing to those in attendance how I had struggled with food all my life until coming to OA. I would tell them how I got a food sponsor and a food plan that worked. I told them how grateful I was to OA for the solution it had given me to a lifelong problem. In my joy and excitement, I wanted everyone to know how grateful I was for this simple, effective, and free program of weight loss.

Much later, I discovered that this euphoric state is well known to those who have been around the programs for a while. It is called *pink cloud abstinence.* Sooner or later, with rare exceptions, it dissolves. It is as though one is given a taste of what is possible, but until he or she does the more difficult psychological and spiritual work, it remains only a sample. When we are new to the program, the support and attention we feel from others, the safety of a structured eating plan, and the availability of meetings and phone contact often help us control our eating behavior. For some, these resources are not sufficient, and when they find themselves unable to follow a food plan they drop out of the program rather quickly. Others, despite difficulty establishing a pattern of abstinence, continue attending meetings hoping one day to become abstinent. Hearing and seeing the success of other people provides encouragement, and so they remain involved with the program support system, hoping thereby to find the strength to control their urges to eat compulsively.

In the first few months, I was able to control my eating in great part due to my enthusiasm for OA. Regular attendance at meetings, phone contact with members, and daily calls to my sponsor lent support to my effort to eat within the guidelines of my food plan. I lost weight quickly and easily. But I had forgotten the significant self-admission I had made that night sitting in my car after the first meeting. In the flush of my successful weight loss, I had forgotten that the essential characteristic that defined me as a compulsive overeater was the loss of the capacity to *control* my eating behavior and weight through conscious effort and willpower.

One day my pink cloud began turning gray. I began cheating on my food plan. Nothing horrendous. An extra helping of cooked vegetables at dinner. A few extra ounces of chicken in my lunch salad. Some days I would tell my food sponsor; other days I wouldn't. During the first months in OA, when I felt the urge to break my abstinence, I would make a program call to keep from acting on the impulse. Now I was giving in to the impulse rather than making the call. Guilt and shame that I had not felt for many months began to return. Food became dangerous again. I began making daily resolutions that, no matter what, I would keep my abstinence, only to retire at night feeling bad because I had failed in my commitment. The program was no longer working for me.

In my desperation, I telephoned a man I had seen and heard at meetings who had always impressed me with his warmth and clarity of thought. He was a black man in his early fifties, and he always had something interesting to impart when he spoke. What he said about the program made sense to me, and when he shared some difficulty or struggle in his life, he demonstrated an openness and maturity that attracted me. I called him hoping that he might offer some guidance. Perhaps he could tell me something that would save me.

When he answered the phone, I sheepishly told him I was having trouble staying abstinent. He listened as I explained that I wasn't sure the program was going to work for me. When I finished speaking, he said that he understood my concerns—he had gone through similar phases during his years in OA. He then offered to help, and I assured him I was interested in what he had to say. He asked if I had been reading the Big Book of Alcoholics Anonymous and working the Steps.[1] I replied that I hadn't really gotten into it much. The truth was, I had skimmed the first few chapters during the first month I was in the program, had found it poorly written and not relevant to my situation. It was about alcohol, and I didn't have a problem with drinking. In addition, I found the language sexist and provincial. After a cursory reading of the first few chapters and some of the personal stories in the back of the book, I put it away on a bookshelf to gather dust. What could I expect to learn from a book by a group of Christian drunks writing about God in the 1930s?

My new program guide recommended going back to the Big Book and reading it again, this time more slowly. He offered to be my Step sponsor, explaining that if we worked together, he would not be interested in what I did with food. I thought that rather odd, given the fact that I understood the whole purpose of OA was to help us control our eating. He explained that, rather than focusing on food and eating plans, he would help me work through the Twelve Steps. He said that when I read the Big Book, I should substitute the words *compulsive overeater* and *food* for *alcoholic* and *alcohol*. I thanked him for being willing to sponsor me and agreed to read the first few chapters of the Big Book to learn more about alcoholism and its relationship to compulsive overeating, and to prepare for taking Step One.

The first Step in every Twelve Step program is the admission of powerlessness over the urge to use some substance or repeat some behavior reason suggests is harmful. Whether it be drinking, compulsive overeating, spending, gambling, or compulsively attempting to control other people's thoughts, feelings, and behaviors, the crucial factor is that a person has, with regard to that activity, lost the power of choice. Most people can freely engage in these activities without difficulty because they can stop whenever they feel like it. However, for people who are addicted or otherwise compulsive, what began as a form of recreation or source of temporary relief from uncomfortable feelings has become an essential part of life. The capacity to control one's behavior is lost. The addict is increasingly dependent on the activity or substance, and life without the temporary relief it provides becomes unbearable.

Recognizing the harmfulness of continued engagement in the activity and sincerely resolving to abstain does not help. The fortunate ones realize this truth, but, tragically, others never do and, instead, go crazy or die, never knowing the nature of their condition. Why is it that people who are addicted or otherwise compulsive cannot control their behavior with regard to the particular substance or activity? And why, with all the evidence that suggests they cannot control their use or behavior, do they continue to believe that they can?

In the book, *Alcoholics Anonymous, alcoholism* is defined as a physical allergy coupled with an obsession of the mind. The alcoholic presumably has a physical reaction to alcohol different from other people's. When a normal person drinks, he or she has a feeling of calm and ease. There may be a slight sense of light-headedness. But non-alcoholics can choose to stop drinking whenever they feel they've had enough. When alcoholics drink, they have a reaction to the alcohol that includes the inability to experience their limit; they can't stop until they're drunk, unconscious, or there's no more to drink. This reaction, unique to alcoholics, is what is called, in the literature of AA, an *allergy*.

The allergy theory rests on the premise that alcoholics suffer from a biochemical condition that produces, once alcohol is ingested, a peculiar loss of awareness of alcohol's toxic effects, and an inability to stop drinking.

While most of those working in the addiction field subscribe to the allergy theory, there are notable dissenters. Two of those who challenge the physical basis of addiction are Stanton Peele and Herbert Fingarette. In their books, they cite research indicating that social, emotional, and habitual patterns, not physical cravings, drive the heavy drinker to abuse alcohol. Their view of the problem leads both writers to conclude that changing these factors can help heavy drinkers return to social drinking.[2]

But the vast majority of those working in the chemical dependency field, most of whom accept the teachings of AA, believe that to suggest to an abstinent alcoholic that he or she might return to social drinking is extremely harmful and potentially fatal. Such a suggestion fuels the alcoholic's mistaken belief that he or she can drink like normal people. AA teaches that at the heart of the alcoholic's inability to stay sober is this tenacious belief that flies in the face of years of failure—that one day he or she can become a controlled drinker. This obsession can lead the alcoholic to give drinking one more try, often with disastrous consequences.

I am not an alcoholic. I occasionally drink socially, but when I do I never get drunk, and I often leave my drink unfinished. One drink is enough to produce a pleasant feeling, and I have no desire to take another. I make no effort to control my drinking—rather I drink or don't drink purely on the basis of how I feel at the moment. Recovering alcoholics consistently report that such reactions are totally outside their experience; once they start, they cannot be certain how far they will go before they stop.

When it comes to food, however, I can identify with the alcoholic's reactions, because whenever I begin eating on impulse, I cannot be certain how much food I will consume before stopping. Even if alcoholics were not allergic to alcohol, or compulsive overeaters were not allergic to sugar or any other foods, there are sound reasons for believing that the recovery process must be based on a foundation of sobriety including total abstinence.

What drives us to use substances that clearly harm us is the desire for relief from inner tensions and distress. It follows that unless we experience a profound psychic change that reduces the levels of tension and distress, we will return to the substance or activity that provides some relief from these intolerable feelings. Obviously, addicts are not the only people seeking relief from pain and uncertainty. All human beings hope to feel good and avoid unpleasant feelings. What makes us unique, however, is that we have hit on a very effective, albeit *temporary* solution—engaging in a specific activity or ingesting a particular substance that alters our mood, thereby relieving our distress.

Unfortunately, we have come to *depend* on this quick solution, rather than experiencing and integrating many of life's difficult challenges. As a consequence, we never fully matured. Abstinence is necessary for us, not just because of an allergy to alcohol or sugar, but because only when we begin experiencing life without resorting to quick fixes are we able to grow psychologically and spiritually. This is why coming to terms with my addiction must eventually involve spiritual work, the essence of which is the willingness to face, rather than avoid, pain and suffering.

The big question isn't why alcoholics can't stop drinking once they start; it's why anyone whose experience would convince reasonable people that they can't control their drinking, would take that first drink *long after being alcohol free.* In other words, it isn't as important to know why alcoholics can't drink moderately, as it is to understand what leads them to take that first drink when all of their experiences indicate that they can't without causing harm to themselves and those around them.

This is the question that had plagued Dr. William Silkworth before he met Bill W.[3] After years of treating alcoholics, Silkworth concluded that some people, after detoxification in a hospital, were capable of abstaining from drink when armed with facts about their vulnerability to alcohol. Other people, however, would invariably return to drinking, even though they had been thoroughly detoxified and taught the dangers of attempting to drink moderately. The former group could be said to have a drinking problem: once they stopped drinking, the problem was gone. But the latter group Dr. Silkworth labeled *true alcoholics* and he had come to believe that they were beyond medical help. Then he witnessed the success of his patient Bill W., who was remaining sober by working with a small group of other alcoholics to help yet other alcoholics by introducing them to a set of spiritual practices. So, when the Big Book was being written, Dr. Silkworth agreed to lend his name in support of the program of recovery outlined in its pages.

Here was an experienced doctor, a specialist in alcoholism treatment, admitting that, despite his extensive medical knowledge and experience, he had been unable to keep alcoholics from returning to the bottle. He could get them clean, but they could not remain sober. He believed the founders of AA had discovered a solution to the problem of how to keep alcoholics from returning to drinking where strictly medical measures had failed.

He reached his conclusion about the effectiveness of the spiritual program of AA based on his observation of the changes taking place in the group of alcoholics who were doing what had previously seemed impossible—maintaining long-term sobriety. It was his opinion that a profound psychic transformation produced by working the Twelve Steps made it possible for these people to *remain* clean and sober.

The first part of Step One in Overeaters Anonymous says, "We admitted we were powerless over food . . ." On close investigation, I have come to conclude that it is not food over which I am powerless. Rather the First Step in embarking on this program of recovery is for me to recognize my incapacity to resist the impulses and temptations to eat that arise in my mind without regard to physical hunger.

The second part of Step One is the further admission "that our lives had become unmanageable." At first glance, I thought I was required to admit that my *eating* made my life unmanageable. But I think this Step requires an even more profound admission: *that my life had become unmanageable because I had come to act in opposition to the realities of life, and could not tolerate the normal frustrations and discomforts that mark human existence.*

Experiencing life as unmanageable drove me to seek the comfort of food. If I felt disgruntled about something or irritated by someone, sooner or later having a snack seemed like a great idea. Behind that seemingly innocent thought were powerful feelings of discomfort and tension. I believe that this is the true nature of my "dis-ease." At some time in my life I discovered eating could calm and comfort me, and I came to depend on food to distract me from real and imagined troubles. Even though I knew in my saner moments that this kind of eating invariably made me fat, whenever I felt the overpowering urge to eat, I forgot that one compulsive bite is too much. No amount of food could satisfy my hunger.

So the habit formed. Once the compulsive patterns become fixed, whenever I began a round of compulsive overeating I was rarely conscious of the underlying feelings of distress. All I knew at the moment was that I needed to get food into my mouth and into my stomach. I was unable to resist the voice within screaming, *I want it now.* When that voice began droning, demanding, or sweetly seducing, I forgot my resolve and it was only a matter of time before I would weaken. As I reached for the chips or the cookies, I tried comforting myself with words I never really believed: *All right, go ahead and eat. Maybe this time you'll have just one.*

* * *

In this First Step, I was forced to confront the truth of my powerlessness. My utter despair, brought about by a lifetime of failed diets and perpetual weight gains, destroyed the tenacious delusion that I had the power to control my food consumption. I had lost even the hope that a diet plan or program sponsor could keep me from compulsive eating. This was the experience AA's call *hitting bottom.* The Twelve and Twelve says, "We perceive that only through utter defeat are we able to take our first steps toward liberation and strength. Our admissions of personal powerlessness finally turn out to be firm bedrock upon which happy and purposeful lives may be built."[4]

The journey of transformation begins out of defeat—the collapse of our faith in the ego alone to solve our eating problem through willpower and reason. William James spoke of this experience as the foundation of spiritual awakening—the collapse of all hope, the experience of total despair. Having come to the point of utter defeat in my eating compulsion, I was open at last to the suggestion that I might find help beyond the familiar human resources of self-will and rational thought.

No single event can awaken within us a stranger totally unknown to us. To live is to be slowly born.
— Antoine De Saint-Exupery

There is a component of our beings, deeper than our personalities, through which we are connected to all beings; and . . . through learning to dwell in this unity of awareness, while still honoring our individual differences, we can experience a love and peace free of fear.
— Ram Dass

Now the real treasure, to end our misery and trials, is never far away; it is not to be sought in any distant region; it lies buried in the innermost recess of our own home, that is to say, our own being. . . . But there is the odd and persistent fact that it is only after a faithful journey to a distant region, a foreign country, a strange land, that the meaning of the inner voice that is to guide our quest can be revealed to us.
— Heinrich Zimmer

CHAPTER TWO

Restoring Sanity

*Came to believe that a Power greater than ourselves could restore us
to sanity.**

The first time I gave any meaningful attention to the Second
Step, I thought, *Well, that's the end of that. I know what they
mean by a Power greater than ourselves. They mean God. I don't believe in God; I never did and can't imagine ever doing so.*

I had continued attending OA meetings despite all the
God-talk I heard. In those early months, I lost weight following my food plan, attended meetings regularly, and called my
food sponsor every day. Whenever someone brought up God
or Higher Power, I merely tuned them out until they passed
on to more practical matters. If others needed to believe in
God to feel better, who was I to argue? I had found the tools
I needed to get my eating and weight under control.

But, having worked through Step One with my Step sponsor, I could no longer avoid the Higher Power issue. The
sources of my resistance were powerful and numerous. There
was my reaction to claims I often heard at meetings that if we
put our faith in a Higher Power (which we all know means

---

* Step Two, the Twelve Steps of Overeaters Anonymous, adapted from the
Twelve Steps of Alcoholics Anonymous. The complete Twelve Steps of AA
appear on page 221.

God), then, in return, God will stop us from compulsively overeating. *How naive,* I thought. Such comments reminded me of the kind of religious thinking that I had rejected as an adolescent when I had been forced by my parents to attend Sunday school. I couldn't accept the idea that there was some conscious Supreme Being waiting for me to believe in Him, who would, in return, bestow on me the gift of removing my urges to compulsively overeat.

Many members of Overeaters Anonymous and other Twelve Step programs seem to understand God as the good Father who gives the gift of abstinence or sobriety to his devoted children and faithful servants. This approach to spirituality grows out of the predominant religious traditions in our culture. In these traditions, God is commonly seen as a transcendent Being capable of granting or withholding His grace as He sees fit. Since I could not accept this religious concept of a Higher Power, I found myself stalled at the gate on my spiritual journey. Believing I had to perceive God in a particular form proved to be a tremendous barrier to my spiritual progress.

Despite repeated statements throughout program literature encouraging me to develop my own personal understanding of a Higher Power, I continued to struggle. Since I did not have an inner sense of a Higher Power and was not comfortable with what organized religion offered, the only way I felt I could press forward was to begin at the beginning. So I embarked on an extensive study of the world's religious and spiritual literature. I began with what was right in front of me, the program literature, especially the Big Book and the Twelve and Twelve.

Reading the Big Book and other sources describing the early history of AA, I came to admire the wisdom and foresight of Bill W., Dr. Bob, and the other early AA members. Recognizing the extent of their struggles with spiritual questions, they agreed that presenting particular theological ideas to prospects was unwise. They understood that any actions that even bordered on preaching a particular concept of God would alienate potential members. Therefore, to create an environment in which newly sober alcoholics might feel safe enough to begin exploring their potential for spiritually based living, AA's founders encouraged new members to develop their own concept and understanding of a Higher Power.

I was comforted by my discovery that many of those who started AA came into the program without belief in God and that several harbored an unequivocal disbelief. In fact, an entire chapter of the Big Book is titled, "We Agnostics." It reflects the difficulties many original members of AA had in dealing with the suggestion that one develop a belief in a Higher Power. Further, it seeks to ease the newcomer's way by advising that all that is necessary to begin the journey of recovery is *some* concept of a Power greater than oneself.

The Twelve and Twelve says that all we really need is the *open-mindedness* and *willingness* to investigate; we do not have to believe anything at first. I began simply with the idea that the person I knew myself to be could not stop compulsively overeating. If some force or power existed that could awaken my capacity to refrain from compulsive eating, it clearly had to be greater than my conscious will. Starting from this premise, I began a personal odyssey through teachings of both Eastern and Western spiritual traditions in search of this mysterious Higher Power. I'll be sharing what I learned throughout this book. Before discussing what I discovered about this subject, I want to examine the second part of the Step.

The second part of Step Two refers to the idea that a Higher Power might restore one to sanity. Upon entering Overeaters Anonymous, I thought the insanity of compulsive overeating referred to my crazy ways of obsessing about and consuming food. Therefore, it was quite natural for me to interpret this Step as meaning that a Power outside myself would make me stop bingeing. It seemed reasonable to think that the word *insanity*, as used in Step Two, referred only to my crazy thoughts and behaviors regarding food. But I have since come to a different understanding of the nature of my insanity.

The first three pages of Chapter Five of the Big Book are often read aloud at Twelve Step meetings as part of the opening ritual. These particular passages explain how the recovery process works and present the Twelve Steps, which are suggested as part of a program of recovery. The attitudes of honesty, open-mindedness, and willingness are described as essential if one is to follow the Twelve Step path. The passage, as usually read, concludes as follows:

> *Our description of the alcoholic, the chapter to the agnostic, and our personal adventures before and after make clear three pertinent ideas:*
> *(a) That we were alcoholic and could not manage our own lives.*
> *(b) That probably no human power could have relieved our alcoholism.*
> *(c) That God could and would if He were sought.*[1]

A very important term here is *alcoholism*. The passage does not suggest that only a superhuman force can prevent the alcoholic from taking a drink. Such a statement would be false. After all, physical restraint and confinement in a place where alcohol is unavailable can keep one from drinking. Antabuse can make the discomfort of drinking so great some alcoholics might not take a drink. Nor does this passage state that no human power can relieve the allergy to alcohol or even the urge to drink. What the passage does promise is that some Power greater than human, a Power some call God, could relieve a person of *the condition called alcoholism*.

Alcoholism is only superficially a matter of excessive drinking, just as compulsive overeating is only seemingly about overeating and obesity. These are merely symptoms of a more fundamental condition related to one's beliefs and experience of the world. As we saw in our discussion of Step

One, the person who is an addict, or otherwise compulsive, views the world through certain attitudinal and perceptual lenses that distort his or her perception of reality and thereby contribute to emotional distress and unhappiness. I believe this distorted perception of reality is the insanity of alcoholism or compulsivity.

Gregory Bateson presents a marvellous explanation of alcoholism and his understanding of the effectiveness of AA in helping the alcoholic to live a sober life.[2] He explains that alcoholism and other compulsions arise out of belief systems and thinking patterns rooted in the minds of those suffering from these conditions. He argues that the alcoholic's problem is not an allergy to alcohol, but rather his or her thoughts and beliefs regarding life and human experience.

Alcoholics suffer from what Bateson calls an *epistemological error* (an error in what they know and how they know it). They see the world through a faulty "body of habitual assumptions or premises implicit in the relationship between man and environment." When sober, they experience the pain and suffering of believing they are separate and distinct from others and the world. At the same time, they hunger painfully for the sense of transcendent consciousness— yearning for the mystical experience that the esoteric teachings of the world's religions call *union with God*, an experience that brings psychic transformation.

Unfortunately, says Bateson, alcoholics hold deep unconscious attitudes and beliefs that prevent them from entering that place of spiritual peace. Instead, they choose the shortcut of alcohol and drunkenness. They see other people as unfriendly forces that must be controlled and somehow neutralized. Weapons such as dishonesty, secrecy, manipulation, and emotional blackmail serve to protect the alcoholic from a hostile world. This sense of alienation, in turn, leads to feelings of insecurity and inadequacy. These feelings are familiar to all human beings, not just alcoholics and other compulsive people. Many thinkers believe alienation to be a natural aspect of the human condition. But what distinguishes alcoholics is that they have found an apparent solution. Alcohol works to bring about a shift in consciousness, allowing them relief from suffering and a taste of the ecstatic—a direct experience of the underlying unity of all things. Viewed in this way, alcoholism can be understood as a misguided attempt, arising out of unconscious spiritual yearnings, to raise the level of one's consciousness.

The Twelve Steps are suggested as a path to alter those deeply rooted attitudes and beliefs (alcoholic insanity). Alcoholics might satisfy their spiritual hunger through opening themselves to the spiritual force at the core of their consciousness, rather than seeking temporary comfort by altering their consciousness with a toxic chemical. This shift in consciousness is the essence of the spiritual awakening or transformation described by all mystical traditions throughout the ages. On this point, the psychiatrist, Arthur Deikman, writes:

> *The sages describe a Way that leads to a higher level of existence, one infinitely more desirable than the level in which most people conduct their lives. The mystical tradition does not offer therapy in the usual sense of the word, but achieving the goal of mysticism—experiencing the Real Self—is said to cure human suffering because its very basis is thereby removed.*[3]

Dr. Carl Jung made this same point when he terminated his unsuccessful treatment of a chronic alcoholic known to us as Roland H.[4] A wealthy businessman, Roland H. had undergone extensive psychoanalytic treatment for chronic alcoholism with Dr. Jung long before AA had begun. Roland had apparently tried many forms of treatment before taking the radical and expensive course of moving from the United States to Zurich, Switzerland, to undergo analysis with Dr. Jung. He had hoped this famous psychiatrist could help him stop drinking.

However, despite a lengthy depth analysis that gave him significant insights into the origins of his emotional problems, Roland had returned to destructive drinking. Even the eminent Dr. Jung had failed to effect a cure, and when the doctor sought to terminate treatment, Roland was understandably distraught. Having tried everything he could find to free himself from the compulsion to drink, he was now looking forward to a slow, painful alcoholic death, which Jung, pulling no punches, said was inevitable. In his terror and utter desperation, Roland asked the doctor whether there might not be some exceptions to the rule that alcoholics like him invariably drank themselves to death. Jung's response to Roland's question is quoted in the Big Book; it eventually became one of the fundamental concepts underlying the recovery process of Alcoholics Anonymous.

> *"Yes," replied the doctor, "there is. Exceptions to cases such as yours have been occurring since early times. Here and there, once in a while, alcoholics have had what are called vital spiritual experiences. To me these occurrences are phenomena. They appear to be in the nature of huge emotional displacements and rearrangements. Ideas, emotions, and attitudes which were once the guiding forces of the lives of these men are suddenly cast to one side, and a completely new set of conceptions and motives begin to dominate them."*[5]

Alcoholism has a physical component, but the drive to return to drinking arises out of the deep unconscious attitudes and beliefs held by the individual. These beliefs are rooted in the unconscious and are impervious to change through reason and willpower. Knowing they are there and that they generate great suffering is a start, but even knowledge of their existence does not change them. What is required, as suggested by Dr. Jung, is a "vital spiritual experience." By that, Jung made clear he was speaking about a profound change of personality—a psychic transformation. He was not referring to seeing a burning bush or watching angels float through one's bedroom window. Rather he was describing a profound psychic event or process that would alter entirely how one experiences one's self, humankind, and the rest of the universe.

Freud and his followers viewed the unconscious as a repository of biological drives and repressed memories from infancy and childhood. Jung viewed the unconscious as having two aspects. The first he called the *personal unconscious*. This was the same as what Freud described. A second aspect consisted of powerful motivating forces passed genetically from generation to generation. Since these psychic forces are shared by all humanity, Jung called this part of the psyche the *collective unconscious*. Jung believed the collective unconscious motivates and shapes inner life just as sense perceptions influence and shape experience of the material world. Jung agreed with Freud that many neurotic symptoms and other psychological disorders grow out of painful, unresolved childhood experiences. But he also believed that some disorders rise from our failure to bring into consciousness the motivations and promptings of this deeper universal consciousness. And he shared the mystic's belief that a significant aspect of our unconscious expresses an evolutionary thrust toward higher levels of consciousness. When these promptings are frustrated or denied, symptoms result. As Dr. Deikman put it,

> *People whose evolutionary need is frustrated experience a persistent dissatisfaction with the course of their lives. On the other hand, fulfillment of that developmental goal enables people to perceive the meaning of their own lives and purpose of human existence. Thus, in the mystical tradition, meaning is a perceptual issue.*[6]

The Twelve Steps are intended as a path that can lead to transformation in perception. This is how I understand the phrase in Step Two that says we could be restored "to sanity." Through rigorous self-examination, meditation, and other actions suggested by the Steps, one's perception of reality shifts at a level deep within the psyche. Perhaps most significant is the shift in motivation from *egocentric* to *Higher Consciousness*.[7] This is why a spiritual approach to healing is so effective in treating addictions and compulsions. More and more people who are investigating the nature of addiction and obsession/compulsion, both lay and professional, are recognizing the profound truth that Jung understood long ago. The addictive process, he concluded, both contributes to, and is an effort to resolve, the tension and distress generated by a person's failure to draw strength and direction from the promptings of his or her Higher Consciousness.

To the outside world my life appeared as a model of success. In my twenties I had attended law school, passed the state bar examination, and spent several years practicing law. While I was fairly successful as an attorney, I was not particularly happy in that career. After undergoing my own psychotherapy, I decided to leave the law to become a psychotherapist. I returned to school and eventually became a licensed marriage, family, and child counselor. My first position as a therapist was as clinical director of a counseling center for adolescents and families. After a number of years, I left the agency and went into private practice. At the same time, I joined the faculty of a local university, where I taught in the graduate school of psychology. I had the esteem of my colleagues and quickly built a thriving clinical practice.

My family life was also going quite well. My first marriage ended in divorce; but in my early thirties I remarried, and my second marriage was and continues to be wonderful. My wife and I raised two sons from our first marriages. We managed to co-parent with our former spouses and to create a vibrant and loving family together. We had a group of wonderful friends, owned a nice home, and had no serious financial problems. Life was, generally, going my way. Except, of course, for the little problem of my weight and my rather strange eating habits, which I could not manage to alter.

When I began working the Second Step, I thought a great deal about the suggestion that I needed to be restored to sanity. I seemed as sane as anyone if sanity were measured by success in love and work. Nevertheless, my sponsor encouraged me to closely examine particular aspects of my personality and the ways I responded to stress and adversity. Rather than focusing on the external indicators of competence and success, he suggested that I investigate some of my odd habits and characteristic reactions to daily life events. There was, for instance, the problem of other drivers.

Other drivers were constantly driving in ways unacceptable to me on what I thought of as *my* road. Irritation consumed me whenever I had to follow another car. I would suddenly become extremely attentive to the driving habits of the person in front of me and would usually find them unacceptable. Often, I would try teaching the driver a lesson by doing something that invariably endangered both of us. Part of my work with Step Two involved taking a close look at this habitual behavior. What I discovered amazed me.

I noticed a voice speaking in my head in those situations: *Damn, if it hadn't been for that S.O.B., I would have had this road all to myself. And look, he is purposely going slow just to annoy me. It's obvious I'm in a hurry!* Actually, I was always in a hurry whenever I found myself behind any car, anywhere, at any time, regardless of where I was going and whether it mattered when I arrived. Enraged, I would drive right to the rear of the car in front of me, determined to pass the jerk. *Could I get by him before reaching the intersection? Who cared as long as I left him in the dust?* Pulling out and coming alongside of him, I would make an obscene gesture with my hand and then careen past. My heart pounded; adrenaline coursed through me. I felt victorious. At the same time, however, I also felt foolish and ashamed of my actions.

I began noticing the extent to which events and situations irritated me, and I came to see how often I felt other people and the universe were mistreating me. Whenever things did not go my way or proceed as smoothly as I had expected, I was quick to blame something or someone. I was shocked to discover the extent to which I was suspicious of people and certain that they would exploit me.

After years of examining these attitudes within myself and listening to others share their experiences, I have concluded that people who are addicted or otherwise compulsive characteristically look for someone to blame when things don't go according to their expectations. Some blame themselves, some blame others. Most of us do both. When things don't go according to plan, we rarely consider that perhaps we had unreasonable expectations or didn't take into account possible interferences. We do not seem to have sufficient flexibility to handle setbacks and complications. We are like little children with no tolerance for frustration, no capacity to contain our anger, and no capacity to delay gratification.

I do not intend to demean. I know from experience how painful it is to attempt to live as an adult when so much of the time I am under the influence of my infantile ego-mind. Part of working Step Two involves noticing how these immature attitudes affect our dealings with those around us. Acknowledging our insanity means recognizing the extent to which these immature attitudes color our sense of ourselves and our experience.

Many of us are often in a private war with the world, needing to be in control of things we can't control. Terrified of looking foolish and making mistakes, we assume others are just waiting for the opportunity to take advantage of and humiliate us. Living with these attitudes and beliefs leaves us in a more-or-less constant state of distress. We need to realize that the insanity referred to in Step Two refers to how we experience ourselves and the world around us rather than specifically being a description of our compulsive habits.

Having explored the theme of insanity, we are ready to return to the principle issue of this Step—coming to believe a Power greater than ourselves could restore us to sanity.

Reason and logic could never prove to me the existence of God. I could not accept the notion of a God who was an unpredictable Grandfather or King of the Universe. As a young boy, I rejected the concept of a God who waited for human beings to express devotion and then showed his pleasure by altering the natural laws of the universe to answer their prayers.

Therefore, in the beginning I took a suggestion from the Big Book and allowed myself to hold an image of my Higher Power that was rather amorphous. Whenever my mind sought to create a concrete picture of it, I reminded myself of what Hazrat Inayat Khan, the great Sufi, suggested:

> *The most advisable thing for the believer of God is to first make his own conception of God. Since we cannot conceive of something in a form we do not know we develop limited 'pictures' of God. So we may all develop our own limited 'picture' with the knowledge that God is beyond that.*[8]

Despite AA's suggestion that each person develop his or her own concept of God, numerous references to the Christian model occur throughout program literature. For those of us looking for a reason to reject the Twelve Step approach this can often suffice. Many newcomers react with discomfort to descriptions of God as "He" and as the "Creator"; some are uncomfortable with reading the word *God*. However, a person with the perseverance and curiosity to investigate these matters need not reject the program, or assume it cannot be of help, because of the references to this particular concept of a Higher Power. As it says in the Big Book,

> *Much to our relief, we discovered we did not need to consider another's conception of God. Our own conception, however inadequate, was sufficient to make the approach and to effect a contact with Him. . . . When, therefore, we speak to*

you of God, we mean your own conception of God. This applies, too, to other spiritual expressions which you find in this book. Do not let any prejudice you may have against spiritual terms deter you from honestly asking yourself what they mean to you.[9]

Typically, religious movements have formed around the life and teachings of extraordinary human beings like Moses, Buddha, Jesus, and Mohammed—people who had had some kind of enlightenment experience. Each of these men, and many other remarkable men and women throughout history, have pointed to a reality unknowable through the physical senses and ultimately incomprehensible to human thought and reason. Despite superficial differences, they offer remarkably similar ideas and practices designed to enable other people to discover this reality for themselves. Jacob Needleman puts it this way: "Imbedded within every traditional culture there is said to be an 'esoteric' or inner path discoverable only by those who yearn for something inexplicably beyond the duties and satisfactions of religious, intellectual, moral, and social life."[10] The Twelve Step programs take us on that path.

Two terms found in the Big Book and other program literature, "spiritual awakening" and "spiritual experience," will be used throughout this book. They may be foreign or confusing to some readers, as they were to me at first. I found the Big Book appendix titled "Spiritual Experience" helpful. It was added when the second edition was printed in 1955, to clear up confusion about how AA was using this term. According to the appendix, there are two types of spiritual experiences—(1) "sudden and spectacular upheavals" and (2) "what the psychologist William James calls the 'educational variety' because they develop slowly over a period of time."[11] Both are described as "personality changes sufficient to bring about recovery from alcoholism."[12]

My own experience has been of the educational variety. While I have had a number of powerful inner experiences and moments of profound insight into the nature of Being during my years in OA, most of the time I have been trudging a more common path. Slowly and falteringly, without benefit of dramatic psychic events, I have experienced a profound and transforming relationship with my Higher Self. To paraphrase the Big Book, I have "tapped an unsuspected inner resource which [I] presently identif[ied] with [my] own conception of a Power greater than [myself]."[13]

At the heart of working Step Two is our belief that we can develop contact with a Power within that is greater than our ego/mind. *Greater* does not mean separate; it means larger and more inclusive than our restricted self-identity. If we are willing to investigate, to look honestly with an open mind, we begin to sense, ever so tentatively at first, the presence within us of a transformative Power. Sustained by the knowledge that the Power we seek resides within us, or at least being willing to entertain this possibility, we are ready to move on to Step Three.

Enlightenment is not an achievement, enlightenment is a transformation of being. And the achiever goes as well as the achievement.

— Ram Dass

Man alone of all the creatures of the earth, can change his own patterns. Man alone is the architect of his destiny. The greatest discovery in our generation is that human beings, by changing the inner attitudes of their minds, can change the outer aspects of their lives.

— William James

When an individual undertakes to bring his life into relation to God, he is embarking upon a serious and demanding task, a task that leaves no leeway for self-deception or illusion. It requires the most rigorous dedication and self-knowledge.

— Ira Progoff

Integration means the creation of an inner unity, a center of strength and freedom, so that the being ceases to be a mere object, acted upon by outside forces and it becomes a subject, acting from its own "inner space" into the space outside itself.

— E. F. Schumacher

CHAPTER THREE

Making a Decision

Made a decision to turn our will and our lives over to the care of God as we understood Him.*

Bill W. might have had someone like me in mind when he wrote, "To every worldly and practical-minded beginner, this Step looks hard, even impossible."[1] Through a great deal of study and self-reflection, I had opened only the tiniest bit of belief that a Power greater than myself existed and could restore me to sanity as suggested by Step Two. However, I was altogether unprepared for what Step Three seemed to suggest. I wanted to be restored to sanity, rendered capable of thinking in new ways so I might be able to live without eating compulsively. Still, it seemed just as crazy to turn my life over to some force whose existence I doubted. And even if such a Power existed, the idea that it had nothing more important to do than help me with my eating problem seemed absurd.

Intellectually, I was beginning to entertain the possibility that there might be a source of guidance and strength deep in my unconscious. But I was not about to turn my will and life over to it. I imagined how friends and colleagues would

---

* Step Three, the Twelve Steps of Overeaters Anonymous, adapted from the Twelve Steps of Alcoholics Anonymous. The complete Twelve Steps of AA appear on page 221.

react when they asked what was new in my life, and I responded with, "Not much. Except that I have turned my will and life over to the care of my Higher Power." Nevertheless, I took up the challenge of this seemingly impossible Step.

I've mentioned how, during my first several months in OA, I was put off by talk about God and Higher Power. I was uncomfortable when I heard statements like, "I have been out of work for several months. My sponsor suggested praying to God for help every morning, and just today I got a call offering me a job. What a miracle! I know the program works, and I'm grateful to my Higher Power for helping me get that job." Hearing comments like that, I asked myself, *How long do I have to continue attending these meetings? Just give me the tools I need to stop compulsive overeating and spare me from having to listen to stuff like this.*

Occasionally, I would speak to someone in the program about my struggles with food or some current life situation, hoping for sympathy and perhaps a suggestion or two. Usually, what I got would be one of the AA slogans such as, Let Go and Let God, or Turn It Over (to your Higher Power). Upon hearing such things, I would smile nicely and say, "Thanks, I should have thought of that myself." Secretly, I would be filled with contempt and irritation, and think this person didn't know what he or she was talking about. After all, I was a successful therapist, trained and experienced in helping others make difficult changes in their lives and in themselves. *I* knew all about effective listening and what to say to someone who was upset.

The suggestions I was being given were definitely not fitting my model of helpful responses. I laughed when I imagined saying to a client who might be experiencing pain over the recent separation from his wife and children, *Hold on there, John. I have a great idea about how you can deal with Mary's decision to leave you and take the kids, the house, and all your money. Why don't you try turning it over to your Higher Power?*

But once I began working through the Steps I became less reactive to what others described as their Higher Power. I was on my own journey of discovery. I turned to my Step sponsor for help with Step Three when it became clear that my resistance to turning my will and life over to God was holding me up. At his suggestion, I read about Step Three in the Big Book and the chapter on Step Three in the Twelve and Twelve. After skimming through the material, I called him, and we made a date to discuss this Step over coffee.

We met one evening in a coffee house, where we took a small table by a large window so we could look out into the night. At several other tables sat small groups of people in quiet conversation. After the waiter brought our coffee, my sponsor asked what sense I had made of the Third Step. Explaining that I had a problem with this Step, I told him I understood it to require turning my entire life over to God. I explained that I didn't exactly believe in God. Furthermore, I didn't think it was a good idea to turn any part of my life over to anyone or anything, let alone something whose existence I doubted.

He sat patiently, eyeing me, a warm smile on his face. When I finished speaking, he asked if I knew the exact wording of the Step. I was irritated by his question; he seemed to be implying that I could not read or remember a simple sentence. His damned smile began to bother me. *Screw you*, I thought. Managing to control my anger, I replied with feigned humility that it said we were to turn our will and life over to God, *as we understand Him*. I put dramatic emphasis on the last part so he would know that *I* understood that we were free to make up our own conception of God. My sponsor continued smiling broadly and said nothing. Obviously, I was missing his point. Then he asked me to read the Step aloud to him. *Jesus Christ*, I thought, *this is ridiculous. Are we playing Dick and Jane see Spot run? I may be a compulsive overeater, but I'm not illiterate!*

I pulled out my copy of *Alcoholics Anonymous* from my carry pack. It did not have the usual blue-and-white cover with the words *Alcoholics Anonymous* on it. Shortly after beginning to read the book seriously, I threw away that cover, replacing it with the dust jacket from Erik Erikson's *Identity: Youth and Crisis.* That way, I would avoid being seen with the book, lest anyone think I might be an alcoholic. Now, with obvious irritation, I opened to page 59 and began reading the Step: "Made a decision to turn our will and our lives over to the care of God *as we understood Him.*" I waited.

"Do you understand what the Step is suggesting that you do?" he asked.

"Obviously not," I responded.

He explained that each Step involves an action. The action called for in Step Three is *the making of a decision.* One is not told to turn anything over to anybody. We decide to change the basis on which we've lived our life, he explained, but the change itself comes through working the remaining Steps and through a future of actions and choices. While I was in no way ready to turn my will and life over to some Power I had only recently begun to consider existed, I was willing to begin taking measures that might slowly lead me into this new life. When our meeting ended, I walked him to his car. As we stood together in the cold air saying good night, I realized how grateful I felt toward this man.

During the weeks that followed our talk, I thought and read about the theme of *decision* in spiritual and mystic traditions. *Metanoia* is a Greek word meaning "turning." It refers to a complete transformation of one's way of being, including the motivations on which one acts in the world. Both the Old Testament and New Testament are filled with stories of men and women who had been living ordinary lives when some powerful and mysterious event occurred, transforming them and leading to the establishment of a new relationship between them and their God. Moses, unaware that he had been born a Jew, was living as an Egyptian shepherd, tending his flocks in the mountains, when God appeared as a burning bush, commanding him to lead his fellow Israelites out of Egypt. Paul, a Jewish rabbi, had been fighting furiously to destroy the early Christian movement when he was struck blind on the road to Damascus. Having had this spiritual experience (conversion), he began carrying the message that the spirit of Christ could be found within each human being. These stories, whether historically accurate or mythic in nature, describe the transformative power of a brush with the Divine in the lives of these reluctant individuals.

The spiritual awakening promised in the Big Book is an experience of *metanoia*; it is a process of psychic death and rebirth into a new way of life. It occurs in the unconscious, independent of intention. On one hand, one may have such an experience without effort. It usually comes in a startling and dramatic moment. Because it has neither been sought nor expected, the event is often extremely unsettling. It often seems to the individual that he or she is going crazy.

On the other hand, one may work tirelessly toward a spiritual awakening by engaging, with great resolve, in various religious rituals and practices. Such efforts may or may not bring about the desired goal. If they do, the spiritual awakening might come as a moment of enlightenment or, more commonly, as a slow, evolutionary process. While Bill W. had a sudden enlightenment experience, most of us working the Twelve Steps have the "educational variety" described in the Big Book. For us, Step Three is the essential act of decision—consciously electing to pursue a course of action intended to produce a new level of consciousness, a new way of relating to life.

Teshuva is a Hebrew word meaning "to turn." Unlike *metanoia, teshuva* has a quality of intentionality about it. I think of Step Three as *teshuva*, an act of conscious will, an intentional turning from one path and entering upon another. Coming early in the long process of personal transformation, it is the act of commitment. This commitment may be renewed again and again in difficult times during the journey. But the first conscious commitment to the pursuit of knowledge of God, which usually comes on the heels of the shattering of one's faith in the power of the ego-mind, is a singularly momentous act.

The process of decision making (*teshuva*) was beautifully demonstrated during a psychotherapy session with a client I was seeing. Richard was on leave from the Catholic priesthood because he had met and fallen in love with a woman.[2] For several months before coming to see me, he had been struggling with whether to end the relationship and return to the priesthood or leave the priesthood to pursue his relationship. He had been, by his account, a good priest, and as I came to know his intelligence and capacity for compassion, I believed him.

In due course of our relationship, he explained how much he loved performing mass, with its elaborate rituals and beautiful symbols, and delighted in giving sermons. He also found great satisfaction in counseling parishioners and attending to the needs of the Church community. But he also spoke of the years as a seminarian and priest as a period of intense loneliness and frustration during which he yearned to experience love, intimacy, and sexuality with another human being. Despite his efforts to suppress and deny these painful feelings and needs, they continued to surface, preventing him from taking complete pleasure in his calling as a priest. One day he met a woman to whom he was irresistibly drawn, and after a time they fell in love.

Falling in love brought his perpetual but submerged conflict into the open, initiating a period of difficult and painful inner struggle. Richard obtained a leave of absence from his spiritual order to give himself time to resolve his raging emotional battle. However, as time passed, he continued to grapple unsuccessfully with his choice. On one hand, the thought of leaving the priesthood was extraordinarily painful. Being a priest fulfilled his sense of purpose and allowed him to serve others and God in a way that seemed ideal. On the other hand, the experience of loving and being loved by one special person was so profound and healing that the pain he felt at the prospect of giving up his relationship was equally unbearable. Richard entered therapy hoping to resolve his conflict and get help in making a decision that would radically affect his life.

For many months he seemed to be getting nowhere. While he had brought to the surface a number of important themes in his life and had done important therapeutic work, he remained unable to reach a decision. One afternoon, he came in for his session saying that he had no ideas about how he wanted to use the hour. This was unusual for Richard, as he always came to sessions with specific issues he wanted to explore. He said he was tired of going around and around about whether to return to the priesthood and was beginning to think his situation was utterly hopeless, that he would never be able to decide.

In an effort to help Richard break through his impasse, I asked if he was willing to work with a guided fantasy. He agreed. Suggesting he close his eyes and go inside himself, I asked him to envision two roads in front of him, one leading to the priesthood and the other leading to the relationship with his lover. As he let the images form, he saw the priesthood road as empty. It dipped down on the horizon, thus preventing him from seeing its continuation. On the other road, he saw his lover waiting for him to make his decision. As his fantasy unfolded, he began moving slowly toward his lover. When he reached her, they embraced. As he spoke, he began to cry, explaining to me that he was crying out of joy over feeling so deeply loved by another human being.

After a time, I asked him to let the fantasy continue. He then reported that his lover was inviting him to continue walking with her, but he was feeling pain and fear over leaving the priesthood. Immobilized by his emotions, he pulled away from his lover and huddled under a large tree. His lover then disappeared, leaving him alone in his anguish.

Again, I suggested allowing the fantasy to continue. He became very quiet for a time. Suddenly, his whole body shuddered and he quickly covered his eyes with his hands. He began wailing. I sat silently, resisting the impulse to take some comforting action out of my own need to ease Richard's pain. After a time, he grew quiet and then explained that in his torment he had torn at his eyes, blinding himself.

He continued. Wandering down the road, he groped his way until he reached the edge of a cliff. He stood looking down into the valley below and then suddenly threw himself over the edge. I asked him what he was experiencing as he fell, suggesting he not worry about conforming to reality. He reported that he was floating slowly down through space, feeling incredibly free and expansive. He continued floating downward, and when he finally landed he found himself back at the fork in the road where the fantasy began. This time he was sitting on the ground in a lotus position. He had recovered his eyesight and once again saw the two roads stretched out before him.

This time the priesthood road had many people on it. They were looking at him expectantly, apparently eager for his return. Richard was happy to see them and moved by their obvious love for him. Then he looked toward his lover on the other road and saw her also looking at him with love and tenderness. Slowly, he stood and once again went to his lover. This time, however, he could not move toward her without acknowledging the presence of the people he was leaving behind. He had to confront their anger, grief, and sense of betrayal. He had to face the sadness, disappointment, and fear they felt in reaction to his abandonment of them. He had to feel his own sense of loss, guilt, and shame. With extreme difficulty, he remained in the fantasy, standing with his lover, listening to members of the community share their feelings of loss and disappointment. Some were weeping, others were filled with anger.

Richard listened and for a time he remained very tense, defending himself from fully opening to the pain. Finally, he spoke to the people, expressing his sorrow that he could not be their priest.

Suddenly, he began crying again; tears flowed down his cheeks and, for some time, deep sobs shook his body. Finally, he grew quiet, his body relaxed, his face free of its customary tension. He told me he saw Jesus standing in front of him and his lover looking lovingly at them both. Jesus was telling Richard that he loved him very much, recognized his happiness at having this relationship, and wanted that for him. Then Jesus rose away slowly dissolving into light. My patient looked at his lover with the recognition that the love they shared was a reflection of the love God had for all human beings.

Richard and I sat quietly for a time, savoring his experience. As the session came to an end, we both recognized that a decision had been reached.

Within a few weeks, Richard began living with his woman friend and shortly thereafter sent a letter to the head of his order stating he would not be returning to the priesthood. He eventually enrolled in a Ph.D. program that would allow him to combine his interest in spirituality, psychology, and the use of myth and storytelling in physical and emotional healing.

He still misses being a priest in many ways and will grieve his loss for some time. But he has made his choice and is now engaged in the long process of integrating his new identity.

Richard's fantasy work exemplifies the elements of decision making of the kind called for in Step Three. It demonstrates that both conscious and unconscious elements are woven into such a profound act of choosing. He began with his conscious mind—with sight. At a certain point he felt the limits of logic and reason; he felt powerless to force a choice. He had to give up his sight and abandon the familiar vehicles of practical planning and rational thought. Jumping off the "cliff," he surrendered to the unknown, experiencing the freedom and power of letting go of his reliance on reason and self-will. In the darkness of his despair he relinquished those tools, and, by so doing, freed himself to find another source of inspiration and direction within. The choice was still before him, but he had new eyes with which to find his way.

The Third Step, read literally, appears to call for giving up all responsibility for one's actions and life to a supernatural source. It is this narrow interpretation that leads to one of the strongest objections leveled at the recovery process and the Twelve Step programs. Unfortunately, the wording of Step Three without further explanation lends itself to this misinterpretation. An in-depth reading of the program literature, principally the Big Book, makes clear that this Step is not an invitation to passivity and irresponsibility. Quite the contrary, Step Three, expressive of the recovery process as a whole, calls upon the individual to take personal responsibility for his or her life choices.

How can we resolve this apparent contradiction? If we are deciding to turn our will and life over to the care of a Higher Power, are we not giving up personal responsibility for ourselves? Help in answering these questions can be found by a close reading of the Big Book's discussion of the nature of the human psyche. Drawing upon the wisdom of the great spiritual traditions of both the East and West, it describes the *human psyche* as consisting of two aspects. One is the ego— our everyday sense of ourselves, who we think of ourselves as being. It is through this ego-self that we meet the world and seek to ensure the satisfaction of our basic human needs. So long as we understand that the ego-self is only a part of who we are and not all that we are, we can develop a healthy and flexible ego. However, when we identify exclusively with our ego, we become disconnected from a deeper, more powerful aspect of ourselves. This other aspect of the human psyche is a more encompassing, though less conscious part. This Higher Self or Higher Power is the true center of the psyche. By connecting with this larger aspect of ourselves, we discover our true nature. We realize that we have an ego, but we are not the ego.

The Big Book explains that this misidentification with the ego is the root of the alcoholic's difficulties. The fundamental problem is not alcohol, we are told, but *egocentricity*—the mistaken belief that the ego is the center of one's being. The cause of our suffering, our sense of isolation, fear and anger at life, grows out of our *egocentricity*. To the extent we remain in the darkness, seeing ourselves as isolated egos, driven by the need to protect this fragile self, we live diminished and anguished lives. In addition, driven by our egocentricity, we engage with the world and those around us in ways that cause pain and suffering to ourselves and those with whom we come in contact.

For example, common to most alcoholics and other addicts is the deep-rooted conviction that we know what's right for ourselves and others in every situation, and that if only we could find the proper tool or technique, we could make things go the way we want. We believe that if others followed our advice and plans for them, all of us would be just fine. Whether we bully others or manipulate them through guilt, we assume that we know what is right and best; in short, we are forever playing God.

Another example of our egocentricity is the pervasive belief that other people have only one function: to meet our needs, or to frustrate our attempts to obtain satisfaction of those needs. For most of my life, it often seemed that other people were nothing more than cardboard cutouts like those sometimes used for crowd scenes in low-budget Hollywood films. These cardboard figures had only one role, to notice me and respond with favor or disfavor. This attitude toward others may seem to imply that I felt a sense of omnipotence, but in fact it shows how much fear and vulnerability I felt. It produced an insensitivity and indifference toward people that often led to behavior in me that offended others and caused them to treat me with the very hostility I feared in the first place.

Working Step Three, I came to understand that *my attitudes* were the soil out of which my compulsive behavior grew. So long as I was motivated by the desire to protect and enhance my ego, I was going to live in conflict and tension with other people and within my own psyche. I was beginning to understand that I had to shift my exclusive identification with my ego, and to see that I could experience a Higher Self where these self-serving attitudes were no longer functional.

Despite my emerging understanding, however, I was still uncomfortable with the language and imagery of the AA literature, which seemed to me to express the religious belief of white Protestant men writing in the 1930s and 1940s. Some of the basic tools and principles were borrowed from The Oxford Group, an evangelical Episcopal organization that sought to rekindle the spirit of early Christianity. They were partly responsible for the AA concept that drunks could find sobriety through spiritual rebirth.[3] To go forward on my own Twelve Step journey, I had to disregard these personally objectionable elements of the Big Book and other program literature in pursuit of the universal truths I sensed were buried just below the surface.

I was helped greatly in this effort by the work of Joseph Campbell, who had devoted his adult life to a study of comparative mythology. According to Campbell, myths and spiritual teachings have two aspects.[4] First, there is a *local element* that speaks to the community out of which the myth arises, with a style and imagery familiar to that community. For instance, the local mountain peak may be representative of the center of the universe or the dwelling place of the gods. Second, there is the *universal element* of the myth or symbol that is expressed through primal universal images rooted in the unconscious of all human beings. So, the mountain in the myth can be interpreted as a universal *expression* of the power and majesty of the forces of the spirit.

In order not to become bogged down in irrelevant local custom and superstition, those wishing to travel the sacred paths must find a way to extract the universal message while leaving the culture-bound aspects to those for whom it might more appropriately serve a function.

This is the universal aspect Aldous Huxley was talking about when he used the term *perennial philosophy*. Huxley wrote of a universal set of beliefs, experiences, and practices underlying all of the great spiritual traditions.[5] Perhaps most fundamental is the idea that behind the world of sensory experience and thought is a *Universal Consciousness*. This Consciousness, which is what many people call God, can be approached and experienced through rigorous and systematic inner work that brings one behind the world of the senses and the world of thoughts. While practices differ from culture to culture, this demanding effort has three universal features that are also built into the nine Steps following Step Three. Briefly, these are (1) working to reduce those factors of our personality and nature that interfere with our ability to contact the Higher Power that resides within our psyche; (2) engaging in actions that bring us into contact with our Higher Power; and (3) allowing our actions to be motivated and directed from this Higher Power (doing God's will).

The Twelve Steps can therefore be seen as a practical guide to incorporating the perennial philosophy into one's life. They can be undertaken without reliance on any formal religious organization or teachings.

Carl Jung, who was very interested in the perennial philosophy, seemed to be attempting to merge psychology and spirituality. For this reason and because he had played a significant part in the early development of the AA program, I began a rigorous investigation of his work. Jung spoke of *archetypes*, which he described as deeply rooted patterns or constellations in the unconscious. An essential part of human consciousness, they pass like basic human physical characteristics from generation to generation. Human beings are born not only with common physical characteristics, but also with similar organizing patterns of thought and motivation that Jung classified with descriptive, symbolically charged terms such as *Mother, God, Monster,* and *Hero.* These archetypes are not directly accessible to our conscious thought, but express themselves in myths, art, dreams, psychotic hallucinations, and religious experiences. Jung thought that much of the psychic distress felt by his patients, especially those over age thirty-five, was a sickness of the soul resulting from their loss of connection with the deeper forces and motivations rooted in the collective unconscious.

To discover and fulfill one's purpose in life, to become a mature man or woman, one must follow the path Jung called *Individuation.* This is the lifelong movement toward psychological and spiritual wholeness. It is brought about in part when we form a relationship with the elements of the collective unconscious significant to us, and find the power and strength for continuing psychic growth through that relationship. Notice how similar the Individuation process is to the Twelve Step recovery process. Both require our willingness to examine and integrate the shadow aspects of the unconscious (those that heretofore have been hidden or oppressed, often manifested as character flaws). Both entail drawing strength and guidance from a Higher Power through expansion of consciousness.

For this reason, it is worth examining the psychological process of Individuation as articulated by some of the neo-Jungians. This can provide us with a bridge between some of the psychological models and spiritual models of the human personality.[6] During the early months of life, in the first stage of personality development, a baby lives in a state that appears to be a kind of primitive experience of Cosmic Unity. There is no sense of self as distinct from others; the mother or primary care-giver is not perceived as separate. Rather the newborn seems to experience only vague sensations of pleasure and displeasure and does not yet conceive these sensations as specific experiences like hunger or satiety.

The second stage of personality development involves separation of ego and Self. The ego here is characterized as the conscious, active aspect of a person's being. It is the psychological vehicle the child uses to engage the world. A self-identity and personality are then formed out of the person's experience and history. The *self-identity* is the inner sense of who one is and the *personality* is the self that is drawn to the world. Parts of the self, which are thought to be unacceptable, are hidden away in the Shadow. We will have more to say about the Shadow later.

The *Self*, as distinct from the ego, is the principal organizing archetype of the human being. Whether Self is motivated and guided by a transcendent source of wisdom and consciousness is not a question I can answer. For me the issue remains open, a wonderful mystery. The fact that I don't know, however, does not hinder my willingness to commit to deepening my relationship with my Higher Self as I understand it at this point.

As the human personality develops through stages in the first half of life, Jung tells us that two processes alternate for prominence in the psyche: (1) inflation and (2) alienation. We commonly think of an inflated person as someone who is taken with his or her sense of importance in interpersonal relationships. These actions are but external symptomatic expressions of the internal psychic process referred to in Jungian psychology as *ego inflation*. Ego inflation is a psychological process or state in which the ego/mind is erroneously identified with the Higher Self. The ego, taken with itself rather than relating as a servant to Self, forgets that Self even exists.

Perhaps the most well-known reminder of the destructive power of inflation comes to us in the myth of Icarus. Icarus's father, Daedalus, was the artist and sculptor who designed the Labyrinth to house the Minotaur for King Minos. Daedalus constructed wings of wax and feathers so that he and his son could fly away from Crete when the father had incurred the king's wrath. Daedalus warned his son not to fly too high nor too low for fear that the heat of the sun might melt the wax or the sea spray might weigh down the feathers. But once they were airborne, Icarus could not contain his exhilaration and flew too high and near the sun. As he approached the sun, the wax melted and Icarus came crashing down into the sea.

Alienation, the other psychic process present in the first half of life, also has popular meanings reflecting our experience with the external symptoms of psychic process. Sociologists use the term *alienation* to refer to social isolation. Philosophers use it when describing those states of being in which the individual cannot find a sense of meaning or purpose to life. Psychologists talk of alienation from one's feelings. What is common among the various uses of the term is the sense that one is cut off from some vital source of energy or meaning. While recognizing all these expressions of alienation, Jungian psychology perceives the source of the symptoms as rooted in the psyche. It is the *loss of connection between ego and Self.*

Both inflation and alienation are natural psychic events. When they begin to predominate our psychic life and are not resolved as we mature, they produce emotional and spiritual dis-ease. When the dis-ease becomes painful enough, it may become the stimulus for our transformation. When the state of inflation, the illusion of omnipotence, can no longer be maintained, the inflated ego collapses, accompanied by feelings of terror and hopelessness. I believe this is what underlies the experience AA calls "hitting bottom." We are potentially ready to heal the alienation of ego from Self.

On one level, Step One is an honest admission that one cannot control his or her drinking. But on a deeper psychic level it is the experience one has of losing faith in oneself. Thinking we were nothing more than an ego, we are terrified at the incontrovertible fact that we cannot manage our life if that is the only resource we have. Until we admit defeat in our battle to control our addictive behavior, we cannot begin the process of recovery. That admission, as the First Step suggests, is *the beginning* of the process. Our inflated ego begins collapsing when we finally face the truth of our powerlessness over our addictive or compulsive behaviors. To admit our life has become unmanageable and that we are not the center of the universe is a crushing blow to the ego. Unless we make this admission, however, and follow it with the actions called for in the remaining Steps, we will continue to vacillate between inflation and alienation. We will attempt to support the ego in its illusion that it is God. At the same time, we will experience shame and wounded pride that result when, through our experience of powerlessness, we are forced to admit that we are *not* God and that we are not even doing very well at just being capable human beings.

Recovery continues in the Second Step when we begin sensing the presence of a Higher Power that resides within the psyche and is separate from ego. Here we begin to address the problem of alienation. Step Two suggests that if we can form a relationship with this Higher Power, *It* will restore us to sanity. We might even say that the acknowledgment that the ego is not the Self, and the recognition that the ego will function better in service of the Self, is the essence of sanity. For once ego and Self can be distinguished, it is possible to establish a working relationship between the two aspects of one's Being, to move toward wholeness. The Self then becomes the source of motivation and power, and the ego, working in its service, no longer must strive to prove it is something it is not.

In Step Three, we commit ourselves to the challenge of developing conscious contact with our Higher Power so that the ego may be placed in service of, rather than in competition with, our Higher Power. My ability to take this Step did not require belief in a Supreme Being, although I do not rule out the existence of such a Being. It does indicate my belief that life will be richer and profoundly more exciting to the extent that I am willing and able to tap the creative power and energy of the Self and bring the ego into its service. Aldous Huxley expressed this idea when he wrote the following passage:

> We know very little and can achieve very little; but we are at liberty, if we so choose, to co-operate with a greater power and a completer knowledge, an unknown quantity at once immanent and transcendent, at once physical and mental, at once subjective and objective. If we co-operate, we shall be all right, even if the worst should happen. If we refuse to co-operate, we shall be all wrong even in the most propitious of circumstances.[7]

Our only enemies are guilt, fear and shame. Such un-resolved negatives prevent us from living fully. . . .
— Elisabeth Kübler-Ross

To get at the core of God at His greatest, one must first get into the core of himself at his least, for no one can know God who has not first known himself. Go to the depths of the soul, the secret place of the most high, to the roots, to the heights; for all that God can do is focused there.

— Meister Eckhart

We do not become enlightened by imagining figures of light, but by making the darkness conscious.
— Carl Jung

CHAPTER FOUR

Writing a Moral Inventory

Made a searching and fearless moral inventory of ourselves. *

Having made the decision to turn my will and life over to the care of God as I understood Him, I now had to act on that decision. The Fourth Step calls for making a *moral* inventory, and I was immediately put off. The word *moral* generated powerful images that caused me to feel a great resistance to carrying out the task.

Morality, and punishment at the hands of authority figures, were inextricably linked in my mind. I recalled physical and emotional punishment I'd suffered as a child as a consequence of engaging in acts unacceptable to my parents and other authority figures. Those acts were often labeled as *bad* or *naughty.* I came to conclude that morality was a set of arbitrary and rigid standards set by those in authority to control those who weren't. As a very young boy attending Sunday school, I developed strong negative attitudes toward the concept of sin as defined by my Sunday school teachers. I balked at the idea that acts people could commit were so displeasing

---

* Step Four, the Twelve Steps of Overeaters Anonymous, adapted from the Twelve Steps of Alcoholics Anonymous. The complete Twelve Steps of AA appear on page 221.

to God that He would punish the transgressor, much as my father punished me when I disobeyed him.

By the time I reached high school I had lost all interest in religion. The final break from organized religion came when I stopped attending the Jewish High Holiday services. These are the most important holidays of the Jewish calendar, during which the Jewish people celebrate the New Year and seek God's forgiveness on a Day of Atonement. The Day of Atonement consists of fasting and praying to God for forgiveness of sins committed during the year, and dedicating one's self to living more virtuously in the year to come. I thought it hypocritical to ask forgiveness at the end of each year when it was obvious that I was going to commit the same "sins" again in the coming year.

This must have been recognized by those who wrote the prayer books because the same prayers asking for God's mercy and forgiveness were clearly going to be read out of the same prayer book year after year. Each time I read the High Holiday prayers, I grew more cynical as I thought ahead to the next year when I would be expected to go through this foolish exercise yet again. I decided to simplify the whole business by admitting once and for all that without a doubt I would do things that were wrong throughout my life and to stop pretending that I thought otherwise. In addition, I saw no point in praying to God for anything, let alone forgiveness for my "sins," because I didn't believe in God any more than I accepted the concept of sin. Thoughts like these led to my total rejection of Judaism or any other formal religion.

Until coming to OA, I had not given much thought to these matters for years, but undertaking Step Four required that I re-examine them. In an endeavor to overcome my strong negative associations to the concept of moral inventories and confessionals, I read the AA and OA literature regarding this Step. In addition, I spoke to many old-timers about their approaches to this Step and read many of the official and unofficial guides to the Fourth Step in print. As the months of research passed, I was becoming quite an authority on how to write a Fourth Step. However, none of my research produced a single written word.

One evening during this period, I happened to turn on the television to watch the news. A reporter was introducing a story about severe rains causing extensive flood damage in the Sierra foothills of Northern California. A camera panned across several houses sitting like boulders in the middle of a river. Cars stood in water up to the bottom of their windows as the news crew, filming from a rowboat, floated through the center of a small community devastated by a swollen river. A middle-aged couple suddenly appeared on the screen. They were extremely upset, yelling at the camera that the government should have done something sooner and brought in pumps or dredges. They announced their intention to sue the government as soon as possible. More shouting could be heard as the television camera began surveying the tragic loss this couple had suffered. Swirling, muddy water filled their living room to a height of about four feet. Chairs, tables, and a sofa floated in the dark water, while fingers of brown wetness crept up the walls. The man and woman continued to angrily heap blame for their woes on "the government." A final close-up photo of the man and woman revealed their understandable rage, fear, and confusion.

The picture on the screen changed. An elderly black man was sitting behind the wheel of an old pickup truck that was partially submerged in the river. Behind him stood his house, destroyed by the flood. As the camera moved in for a close-up of his face, I saw an extraordinary warmth and peacefulness in his eyes; he radiated a calm presence. In my professional work, I have seen many people in a state of shock shortly after a tragic event. They have a look of not being present; they appear lost and confused. But shock was not what appeared on this man's face. It was something very different. I stared at his face as the newsperson began questioning him.

The interviewer asked him how much he had lost. "Just about everything I own," came the man's reply. The newsperson, obviously curious about this fellow, pressed on with his questions, asking how he was managing to cope with such a tragedy. The old man looked directly into the camera. He smiled and began explaining that while it was hard to lose all of his possessions, he considered them all as gifts from God in the first place. He added that he was grateful to God for allowing him to have had a house and his possessions and that he believed God would take care of him in the future. Since God had always taken care of him in the past, he expected God would help guide him through these current hard times. I was transfixed by the peace I saw in this man's face, and I could not get him out of my mind as the news program moved on to other stories.

Later that evening, I pondered the responses of the couple and the old man. Both had suffered terrible losses and were facing a time of painful and difficult transition, and yet their reactions were so different. What distinguished them? What allowed the old man to appear radiant and calm under the same circumstances that devastated the couple? The answer lies in the way each person perceived the crisis. The old man was capable of placing the crisis in a broader context. Even in the midst of tragedy, he could be grateful for the good things he had experienced in his life. And he could rest comfortably in the knowledge that existence is extremely unpredictable and that human beings are often powerless to control major events shaping their lives. He did not blame himself or anyone else for his misfortune; he could still look to the future with hope.

In contrast, the man and woman shown in the first sequence were unable to step back and allow themselves any relief from the distress of the moment. Their anger arose from their terror in confronting the fragility and unpredictability of life. As it would for most of us, a tragedy had brought the disquieting truth into sharp focus for them. And, as many of us would under the same circumstances, this couple sought to reassure themselves that life is orderly, to deny that tragedy can occur without a known cause, that crisis doesn't "just happen." They resorted to one of the universal defenses against experiencing the apparent randomness of events—they sought someone to blame. In this case they pointed their fingers at "the government," thus taking comfort in the fact that *some* force had control and power over events, even if it was not them.

Continuing to reflect on that piece of news footage over the next few days, I realized that a moral inventory might not be so much a process we use to identify evil thoughts and sinful ways. Instead, it might be a way we identify those habits of mind that lead to unskillful ways of responding to inner and outer events.[1] The character defects defined in the course of writing an inventory are habits of mind, deeply ingrained attitudes and beliefs we develop over a lifetime. They are rooted in the millions of major and minor life experiences that establish and reinforce our characteristic ways of reacting to life's highs and lows. Viewing events through these *negative thought filters,* our character defects, invariably leads us to feelings of anger (resentment), anxiety (fear), and guilt or shame.

In OA, I had been learning that so long as my life was pervaded by such painful feelings, sooner or later I would turn to food for the temporary relief it could provide. Once I began eating to alter my mood, in response to an inner compulsion rather than the physical need for fuel, I could not be certain when I would stop. Here was the link between my character defects and my compulsive eating—the pervasive negative feelings generated by the character defects within my psyche. I understood why identifying these attitudes and habits of thought is an integral part of any program promising freedom from compulsive overeating.

Reflecting on that television news story, I reached a deeper understanding of the comments, quoted in the Big Book, that

Carl Jung had made to the alcoholic Roland H. Jung attempted to explain to his despairing patient the nature of a spiritual experience and why Jung believed such experiences had helped other alcoholics. He said, "Ideas, emotions, and attitudes which were once the guiding forces of the lives of these men are suddenly cast to one side, and a completely new set of conceptions and motives begins to dominate them."[2]

With this understanding, I began the task of writing my Fourth Step inventory, having a goal of identifying the conceptions and motives that had been the guiding forces of my life. My sponsor had suggested a format, which I used, with some modification.[3] It consisted of two parts. The first was a secrets list—all the things I had done about which I felt shame and which I had never told anyone. The second consisted of sheets of paper on which I drew four columns. In the first column, I listed the names of people significant to me who made me feel uncomfortable when I thought of them. In the second column, I described briefly the nature of the events involving these people that caused these feelings. In the third column, I named the feelings I still harbored about these people and events. In the fourth column, I recorded the particular attitude, belief, or thought that supported either the harmful feelings I felt in the past, those I continued to carry in the present, or both.

For example, I listed an old friend I resented because he had borrowed stereo equipment, moved away shortly thereafter, and never returned the items. The feelings I listed at once were anger and resentment. Then I realized that fear was also present, fear that if I trusted people I could be exploited. In the fourth column I placed the character attitudes. First was the belief that anyone who mistreated me was unworthy of my care and affection, regardless of the nature of our relationship as a whole or the possible circumstances that might have led the other person to act in "unskillful ways." Second was the belief, reinforced by my friend's failure to return my things, that it was wise to be suspicious of others, to expect the worst. Finally, there was even the belief that since someone had kept things belonging to me, I could do the same to others.

Examining my completed inventory, the first thing I noticed was that regardless of the person or circumstances listed in columns one and two, column three invariably contained a variation of the following feelings—anger/resentment, shame/guilt, or anxiety/fear. My resentments arose because someone had done something to me that I could not forgive. My guilt centered on acts I had committed against others for which I could not forgive myself. And my fears grew out of fantasies spun by my mind concerning possible future events in which I would suffer some loss—financial, emotional, or physical. I then noted that every expression of these feelings described in my inventory was reinforced by a set of beliefs deeply embedded in my identity and world view.

In the feelings column, I had noted old resentments toward people who had done things to me in the past. Years of resentment, buried in my unconscious, surfaced as I recorded the people, situations, and experiences of my life. Now, examining the beliefs and attitudes that generated and maintained those feelings of resentment, I recognized that the people and their particular actions toward me were far less influential in shaping my emotions than the attitudes and assumptions by which I lived. While the names and circumstances kept changing over the years, my attitudes remained the same, consistently producing feelings of anger and resentment.

For example, one of the principal character attitudes uncovered by my efforts was the deeply embedded belief that others always act toward me with conscious intent. This assumption, in turn, led to another belief—that when someone does something I don't like or that in some way hurts me, he or she intends to harm me. My reaction to my friend's failure to return my stereo equipment was but one example. I had no way of knowing what might have been the cause of his failure to return my belongings. Nevertheless, his failure became evidence that people will intentionally harm me if I am kind and generous.

Obviously, many supporting feelings and beliefs, which interfere with the establishment and maintenance of healthy interpersonal relationships, can flow from that one. While it is only common sense to use judgment in trusting others, to assume only the worst hardly leads to a sense of security in our relationships or our desire to cultivate intimacy. Harboring resentments and revenge fantasies for perceived past injustices produces a powder keg of anger ready to ignite whenever anyone fails to behave toward me as I wish. Whether I respond actively with an open expression of anger or passively withdraw, the result is the same: my mistrust of others deepens and my relationships suffer.

The second major feeling after resentment that reappeared throughout my Fourth Step inventory was guilt. Before writing my inventory, I had always assumed I was not plagued by that emotion. It had been so skillfully and completely suppressed in my childhood that during years of therapy such feelings never came to the surface. Whenever my therapist suggested I might be feeling guilty about some unkindness I had done, I became confused. Rather than experience guilt when speaking about nasty or cruel things I had done to others, I felt a kind of deadness, an absence of emotional aliveness. Because my parents often used shame to motivate me to behave in ways contrary to my desires and intentions, and because I'd confused shame and guilt, I developed the ability to protect myself from consciously experiencing guilt. By suppressing all feelings of guilt, as I grew into adulthood I was able to act in unskillful ways while preserving my self-image as a good and kind person. To have felt remorse would have required taking responsibility for hurtful things I had done. However, my inability to experience guilt meant I was incapable of investigating my motivations and feelings deeply enough to bring to the surface the shame and guilt hidden in the shadows of my psyche.

Reviewing what I had written in my Fourth Step inventory, I saw the sometimes cruel and often dishonest things I had said and done to people over the years in anger and frustration. With this recognition came memories and feelings of guilt I had suppressed. This retrospection brought to mind times that I had behaved in mean-spirited, hurtful ways toward service people, colleagues, friends, and intimates. I felt the sickening waves of shame and guilt I had walled off from consciousness all those years. It was an unsettling and painful experience.

In opening this Pandora's box, I had gotten more than I had bargained for, but slowly, with the help of my Step sponsor and a number of friends in the program, I started to accept my feelings of guilt. I was repeatedly reminded that I was in the middle of a larger process and that the Steps to come would help me to resolve and integrate the material I was discovering in my Fourth Step. Facing these feelings of shame and guilt was necessary if I was ever to free myself from their burdensome effect on my ability to enjoy life.

Reviewing my inventory, I discovered that where the feelings of guilt or shame appeared in the third column, the character defect that most often appeared beside them in column four was perfectionism.[4] Perfectionism is the character defect that says: *in order to be worth anything I must never make mistakes.* An expression of pridefulness or grandiosity, perfectionism is a form of ego inflation growing out of the belief that one can and should be without faults. Because I could not accept any flaws in my character or behavior, I was forced either to deny my mistakes or to endlessly experience guilt for things I had done in the past. I had chosen the former on the conscious level but had to bury the guilt in the recesses of my psyche. In this way, I could preserve my ego inflation and maintain the illusion that I was better than other people. Here again, one can obviously see how this character defect, as an expression of egocentricity, leads to fear of others and produces actions that arouse hostility in others.

The third feeling that appeared repeatedly in column three of my Fourth Step was fear. In the character defect column next to fear, I had repeatedly noted my habitual attitude that others were always scrutinizing *me* and *my* activities. I don't mean to create the impression that I was completely paranoid. But I did have this voice in my head, which I often believed, that told me I was the center of attention, even when no one seemed at all interested in my presence. Here was the source of the attitude that others need not be taken seriously except when their feelings and opinions reflected their reactions to me. These character attitudes often led me to behave with insensitivity to the needs and feelings of others, or they led to my extreme performance anxiety, my fear of shamefully failing in public.

Since I carried in my unconscious the belief that I was the center of the universe, other people's thoughts, feelings, and needs tended to be irrelevant except insofar as they related to my desires or needs. This particular constellation of character attitudes—grandiosity and false pride—is quite common among compulsive people. In meetings, one often hears it spoken of as follows: "Before I came to the program, I always thought of myself as the piece of shit around whom the world revolved."

Protecting my inflated sense of self required several strategies, all of which proved harmful. One was to avoid situations in which I might experience failure or appear weak or foolish. It seemed essential to circumvent new situations in which I might experience the awkwardness of being a beginner. Of course, if, despite my best efforts, I did experience the embarrassment of making mistakes publicly, I would often resort to the strategy of blaming someone else or the situation for what had happened. I had to place blame elsewhere to avoid exposing that vulnerable place where I felt shame and inadequacy.

Another strategy was to alter the memories I had of events in support of enhancing my self-image. Recalling events, I would reconstruct things so I appeared more upstanding, honest, and good than might have been the case.

In the days that followed the completion of my inventory, I occasionally picked it up and reviewed what I had written. When I did so I felt a mixture of sadness, relief, and excitement. I saw the names of all the significant people in my life and the important events that had taken place between us. I saw repeated references to feelings of anger and frustration, sorrow and fear. And I reviewed the character attitudes and beliefs that motivated many of my harmful behaviors toward others. And, finally, I reflected on the harmful actions I had taken toward others in an effort to protect or reinforce my ego inflation.

Once I'd completed my inventory, I turned to what I was learning from my study of Western psychology and the great spiritual traditions to find some tools for processing this information in a way that would allow me to change my behavior. I have found that there are methods that can help me in my recovery work, not by fighting to defeat something "bad" in myself, but by accepting and integrating those elements of my psyche that I'd either repressed or misdirected.

For those of us not comfortable thinking of character defects as "bad" or "sinful," it can be helpful to think of them instead as habits of mind that perpetuate suffering. This approach allows us to develop ways of understanding and working with these aspects of our inner life without falling back into the black-and-white thinking that contributed to our difficulties in the first place.

Our psychospiritual growth results from engaging in practices through which our character defects are transformed and integrated. Almost all religious traditions have practices or rituals in which the faithful identify and confess aspects of their inner life that interfere with spiritual health. In the Christian tradition, for example, *purgation* refers to acts intended to purify oneself. It involves identifying one's character defects and becoming willing to have them removed through God's grace in order to enter into a committed and intimate relationship with God. The founders of AA used this model.

Relying on his own experience with Christianity, it was natural for Bill W. to suggest in the Twelve and Twelve that character defects could be thought of as the Seven Deadly Sins, products of egocentricity to be rooted out of one's psyche. If one starts from the premise that character defects are in themselves bad, it follows that one must identify them in a moral inventory to bring about their removal. The sins of pride, anger, sloth, gluttony, envy, greed, and lust are sources of spiritual disease, according to the Big Book, and must be removed because they "stand in the way of our usefulness to God and our fellows."

I have been suggesting another way of approaching one's character defects that has a long spiritual tradition. Interestingly, this alternative is not entirely missing from the pages of AA literature, although it takes a close reading of the program literature to find it. For instance, while Bill W. used many Christian references in his discussion of the Fourth Step in the Twelve and Twelve, he pointed out that there are other equally valid methods of defining character defects. Recognizing that many AA members did not and would not accept a traditional religious approach in these matters, he wrote:

> To those having religious training, such a list would set forth serious violations of moral principles. Some others will think of this list as defects of character. Still others will call it an index of maladjustments.[5]

Later, in the Twelve and Twelve, the suggestion is made that self-centered fear is the chief activator of our character defects. Fundamentally, what we fear is the wounding of our pride and the collapse of our inflated ego. We also fear that our basic instincts will not be satisfied—that what comes to us will be insufficient to satisfy our needs. So we live in opposition to other human beings and the world around us. We are deeply suspicious and self-protective. We are constantly trying to hide what we believe to be a self that is inadequate and vulnerable. Bill W. puts it the following way:

> *Character defects, representing instincts gone astray, have been the primary cause of [our] drinking and [our] failure at life; that unless [we are] now willing to work hard at the elimination of the worst of these defects, both sobriety and peace of mind will still elude [us]; that all the faulty foundation of [our] life will have to be torn out and built anew on bedrock.*[6]

Despite this reading of the program literature on the subject of character defects, it seems to me that AA's predominant approach calls for efforts seeking the destruction and removal of one's character defects. Such an approach, as I have suggested earlier, suffers from the unfortunate potential of splitting the world of the psyche into good and bad, resulting in what many psychologists of religion and moral development call *dependent morality*. There is a danger in taking on the code of others, usually authority figures, out of fear of punishment from outside and feelings of shame within. It can lead to moral rigidity and inability to accept and integrate parts of oneself. What is to me a higher level of moral development involves replacing external moral standards with a more inner-directed sense of which actions are skillful and which are not. This inner morality involves a sensitivity to one's shared human condition and recognition that we are all a mixture of positive and negative human qualities. Since the ultimate goal of recovery is to cease fighting anything, including ourselves, eventually each of us must make the transition from dependent to inner-directed morality. In this way, recovery leads to acceptance and integration of all parts of ourselves. This process results in a reduction of the influences of the more disruptive elements of the psyche.

Buddhism offers such an approach to working with character defects. In the Buddhist tradition, character defects are called *defilements*. They are thought of as ways the human mind attempts to hold on to what is experienced as pleasant and to avoid what is experienced as unpleasant. The list of defilements, which reads much like Bill W.'s description of character defects, includes fear, rigid habits of thought, anger, resistance, and the inability or unwillingness to bring awareness to what is happening moment by moment.

In addition to the defilements, Buddhists speak of five *hindrances to enlightenment*. The first is the desire for (lust) or clinging to (greed) sensory pleasure. It is not the experience of sensual pleasure that causes difficulties; it is the striving of the ego-mind to obtain, control, and maintain sense pleasure.

The second hindrance is *aversion*—the drive to avoid the unpleasant. Included are anger and ill will that arise in our life as we seek to avoid people and situations disturbing to us. It also includes fear, which arises out of the desire to hold on to pleasant experiences and avoid possible unpleasant experiences.

Sloth and torpor, a third hindrance, correspond to the sin of slothfulness in Christian thought. *Sloth* refers to a laziness of mind, an unwillingness to make commitments and follow through on them when things get tough. *Torpor* refers to dullness of mind—our tendency to be inattentive and to lose our focus.

The fourth hindrance is restlessness, both physical and mental. It includes our tendency to fidget and our inability to be quiet for any length of time. It also refers to the mental fidgeting we do in the form of ruminating, worrying, and obsessive thinking. Boredom, which is a form of restlessness, falls within this category.

The final hindrance, doubt, may be the most powerful because, according to Buddhist thought, it can drive one away from the path of enlightenment and recovery. This lack or loss of faith, expressing itself through thoughts, can cause one to abandon the search for his or her Buddha nature.

In the Buddhist tradition the hindrances are neither indulged nor suppressed. A middle path is suggested—the practice of mindfulness: non-discriminating awareness of whatever arises moment to moment, including hindrances and defilements as they arise in the mind. The task is not to fight them but to transform them into objects of meditation. Rather than either applying force of will to suppress the character defects or praying to a transcendent God to remove them, one brings non-judgmental "bare attention" to whatever arises in the mind.

Character defects, which are seen merely as calcified forms of thought, arise in the mind. As they do so they become objects of careful, non-judgmental investigation. As one's ability to maintain awareness grows through the practice of meditation, one begins to notice that egocentric thoughts, like all thoughts, arise in the mind quite by themselves. They float through the mind like clouds, and if one does not grab at them or endeavor to push them away, they naturally pass away, replaced by other thoughts and sensations. This simple, but profound, discovery can help us loosen our identification with the ego/mind and can open us to the discovery that we are an expression of our Higher Power (Buddha-nature) rather than an egocentric self.

Carl Jung was in many ways critical of traditional Christianity. One of his principal objections was the Christian emphasis on the need to root out the dark forces in the human psyche to make way for the light of God. Jung argued that psychospiritual growth can only take place through reconciliation rather than inner conflict and defeat of one psychic element by another.

During my recovery, I have come to believe my spiritual path is one of peaceful reconciliation, both in my encounters with the world around me and within myself. Rather than fighting to rid myself of what seems unacceptable or bad within, I have learned to use the Steps to effect transformation of my character defects and integrate these elements into my consciousness. My goal is to free the energy bound by egocentric fear so that the creative forces behind these fears can be channelled into more healing pursuits. This is the *path of individuation.*

It involves bringing the *Shadow,* the unacceptable elements of the psyche, to the surface of consciousness and acknowledging all of its aspects so that it can be integrated, rather than destroyed. Step Four is Shadow work. Fritz Kunkel, a Jungian psychotherapist and spiritual thinker, puts it this way: "From the viewpoint of depth-psychology and acceptance of the Shadow means honesty and confession, and leads to the experience of forgiveness, which is the only way out."[7] Kunkel goes on to say that our character defects must be acknowledged and accepted so that the creative power hidden behind their harmful aspects "can be consciously accepted so as to make life richer and more vibrant. Forgiveness is reconciliation, and can come about only through recognition of the negative forces that have to be cleansed and accepted."[8]

Thus, the healing work of the Twelve Step programs is a process for becoming whole. The task of integrating character defects begins with acceptance—not judgment and self-loathing. Healing emotional and spiritual wounds requires a gentle, loving awareness. Stripping away our protective defenses against seeing all that we are, we expose warded off aspects of our personalities to consciousness. This work is often extremely painful. In order to go deeply into these parts of ourselves, we need to approach them with the qualities of mercy, compassion, and self-forgiveness. These qualities, even though barely available to us in the beginning of recovery, allow us to move forward on this demanding path of self-awareness and self-acceptance. As we continue in our recovery, we come to understand, through experience, that our spiritual healing is primarily the cultivation of these precious qualities in the human heart. Bearing them in mind eases our way into Step Five.

There would appear to be a sort of conscience in mankind which severely punishes everyone who does not somehow and at some time, at whatever cost to his virtuous pride, cease to defend and assert himself, and instead confess himself fallible and human. Until he can do this, an impenetrable wall shuts him off from the vital feelings that he is a man among other men.

— Carl Jung

A willingness to both look inside oneself and to share that knowledge is essential for self-discovery to occur. And self-discovery is the foundation of personality growth or behavioral change. That willingness to search within, to seek what is there and to share it, occurs best in an atmosphere of security, embracing mutual trust, caring and respect.

— Gershen Kaufman

Once some secrets have come out and been confessed they do not need to be referred to again and again, built into cornerstones for a psychopathology. The aim of confession is lustration; what is washed away is gone, carried off by the river to a far sea. The unconscious can absorb our sins. It lets them rest, giving the feeling of self-forgiveness.

— James Hillman

CHAPTER FIVE

Sharing the Moral Inventory

*Admitted to God, to ourselves, and to another human being the exact nature of our wrongs.**

Having completed my Fourth Step inventory, I now faced the next challenge. Surveying my life to uncover my character defects and acknowledging the unskillful actions motivated by those attitudes had been difficult tasks. But now it was necessary to share all of this with another person. Before I was able to summon the courage to call my Step sponsor, I prepared myself, as was becoming my habit, by exploring the AA literature. Before I could take the Fifth Step I needed to know why it was important to share my written inventory with someone. Wasn't it enough that I identified my character defects and acknowledged the harms I had done under their influence?

Both the Big Book and the Twelve and Twelve stress the importance of sharing the Fourth Step inventory with someone. The message is clear and insistent: If I am to live free of the compulsion to eat compulsively, I cannot keep these matters secret. The Big Book says this to the alcoholic:

---

*Step Five, the Twelve Steps of Overeaters Anonymous, adapted from the Twelve Steps of Alcoholics Anonymous. The complete Twelve Steps of AA appear on page 221.

> *If we skip this vital step, we may not overcome drinking. Time after time newcomers have tried to keep to themselves certain facts about their lives. Trying to avoid this humbling experience, they have turned to easier methods. Almost invariably they got drunk. . . . They had not learned enough of humility, fearlessness and honesty, in the sense we find it necessary, until they told someone else all their life story.* [1]

Once we commit ourselves to sharing our inventory, the next question becomes with whom to do so. The program literature suggests that we select someone who represents authority in our religious community, if we are a part of one. While one's psychotherapist might be suitable, I feel strongly that the Fifth Step should be read to someone who has gone through this process. I believe that while reading it to your therapist can be valuable, reading it to one's sponsor or someone in the program who understands its importance seems the best approach. [2] I hope to make my reasons clear later in this chapter.

Before making my appointment with my Step sponsor, I considered the two other actions suggested by Step Five, admitting my wrongs to myself and to God. The former I felt I had accomplished in that I had reflected on my character defects and the harms I had done to others as described in my inventory.

But what of the suggestion that I admit these matters to God? I had often exposed unflattering aspects of my personality to a trained professional, who is paid to listen without expressing judgment. So in admitting to myself and even to another person my shadow parts I was in familiar territory. But the suggestion that I admit my wrongs to God, as I had initially understood this concept, seemed ridiculous. If God existed and was all knowing, I could never keep secret from this Supreme Being either my motivations or my behaviors. Why, then, should it be necessary to admit my faults to God?

However, as I no longer conceived of God as a punitive parent, I understood that this form of confession was not the same as, when in high school, admitting to my father that I had dented the front fender of his car. My willingness to confess my wrongs to my Higher Power was motivated, not by fear of punishment, nor by the hope I might escape punishment by being truthful, but by the desire to deepen and strengthen my contact with this inner source of power. At this point, I perceived this part of Step Five as another encounter between my ego and Higher Self. Through this encounter, I figured that my identification with ego might be reduced and the alliance between ego and Self enhanced.

Not without some embarrassment, I sat in the quiet predawn hours with my written inventory in hand. I began by silently expressing my intention to acknowledge to my Higher Power the exact nature of my character defects and to admit all of the wrongs done to other people. Then I read my inventory aloud. When I had finished reading the twelve pages of my written inventory, I sat in silent meditation for a while. Nothing dramatic occurred, but I could sense a subtle shift within—some psychic tension was softening. In that moment my body shuddered.

Later that same day, I called my Step sponsor to make an appointment to complete my Fifth Step. I was still very uncomfortable with the idea that I was going to share my darkest secrets with someone who was not professionally trained. I did not even know what he did for a living, nor his educational background. All these things might have meant a great deal to me before I started this Twelve Step work, but now they mattered less. What made him the right person was that he, too, was a compulsive overeater and that over time I had come to trust him. It was important to me that he was no longer plagued by obsessive thoughts about food and weight and so was no longer compulsively driven to overeat. Feeling a little nervous and self-conscious, I called him, and we agreed to meet before an OA meeting we both attended regularly. We agreed to find a quiet spot in the church where the meetings were and gave ourselves a couple of hours for the task.

He was already waiting outside the building as I drove up and parked my car. Feeling very nervous, I got out carrying my inventory in a large manila envelope. We hugged briefly, and I began to relax a little as we set out in search of the right place to read my Fifth Step. Searching the building for a spot where we could carry out our assignment without interruption, we eventually found a small, comfortable room. There was a thick purple carpet on the floor and a few easy chairs casually placed about the room. A soft overhead lamp provided the only light, but it was more than sufficient. I rather liked the fact that the room was not brightly lit. I felt safer, less visible.

We each took a seat, and I immediately pulled my Fourth Step inventory out of the envelope and prepared to read what I had written. Holding the pages in my slightly trembling hands, I was eager to start right in, hoping to race through the reading without pause. My sponsor, however, stopped me and suggested we begin by reading the Third Step Prayer together. I thought to myself, *Isn't this uncomfortable enough, having to read all of this awful stuff, without also having to recite prayers?* But I said nothing that would reveal my resistance to his suggestion, and we began reading the prayer together out of the copy of the Big Book he had brought.

> *God, I offer myself to Thee—to build with me and to do with me as Thou wilt. Relieve me of the bondage of self, that I may better do Thy will. Take away my difficulties, that victory over them may bear witness to those I would help of Thy Power, Thy Love, and Thy Way of life. May I do Thy will always!*[3]

As we read the prayer aloud, I was surprised to find myself comforted by it. By the time we finished, my anxiety level had dropped dramatically.

Then I began reading my inventory. I came to several points where I spoke of things that were very embarrassing and painful to share. When I described things I had done to people who had shown me kindness and trust, I experienced a great deal of shame and wanted to hide my face or bolt from the room. It was hard to admit that, in the past, I had taken advantage of people who had depended on me. There were moments when it was too difficult to go on and I stopped reading. During those painful silences my sponsor merely sat calmly. Experiencing his gentleness and understanding, I pushed forward, continuing to describe motives and incidents from my life that I had always kept secret, many even from myself. Occasionally, he interjected something, once or twice sharing from his own past to ease my mistaken belief that no one else could have done the things I was describing. But for the most part he just listened.

We continued in this vein for almost the entire two hours we had reserved. By the time I had completed my task, I felt as though my sponsor and I had known each other all of our lives. In that brief space of time both of us had revealed many secrets. We had revealed ourselves—our strengths and our weaknesses, our courage and our cowardice. Two human beings—two hearts—touching in healing.

Having completed our work together, we hugged for a moment, then went to join the evening OA meeting that was about to begin. Walking into the large meeting room, I saw twelve or fifteen people seated in a circle. Many of the faces were familiar to me, but in that moment everyone looked unusually beautiful. There seemed to be a light around each person. I took a seat, continuing to look around the room in amazement. Occasionally, I felt tears rolling down my cheeks. I was aware that the constant, pervasive fear I had felt toward strangers was gone, and I was experiencing an incredible sense of peace. I felt as though my heart would burst with love for everyone in the room. I was in such an altered state of consciousness during the meeting that I have no recollection of what was said. I do recall that after the meeting I went home and pulled out the Big Book.

My sponsor had suggested reading two particular pages before going to bed that night as a follow-up to my having done a Fifth Step.[4] Following his suggestion, I turned to the pages he mentioned and started to read. I was stunned. Even though I had read these pages several times in the past, I did not recall ever having noticed the words that now jumped out at me.

> *Once we have taken this step, withholding nothing, we are delighted. We can look the world in the eye. We can be alone at perfect peace and ease. Our fears fall from us. We begin to feel the nearness of our Creator. We may have had certain spiritual beliefs, but now we begin to have a spiritual experience.*[5]

This was what was happening to me. I was not having visions or anything like that. I was not having visitations or seeing miracles performed before my eyes. Rather, I experienced a profound sense of unity with other living beings and the rest of the world. The extraordinary feeling of peace and love I had during the evening meeting I now recognized as an expression of that sense of oneness. It occurred to me that this was what religious people mean when they describe being touched "by the Spirit of the Universe." I also thought of the term used by Abraham Maslow for those momentary events in the lives of some people that open them to new levels of wholeness and peace. He called them *peak experiences.*[6] When I read Maslow in the early seventies, I had thought that he was referring to some profound experience of sensory pleasure, such as sitting under the stars on a clear, cold night in the desert. I now understood that such a sensory experience could *trigger* a peak experience, but the latter happened at a deeper internal psychic level. Completing my Fifth Step was, for me, a peak experience.

Before going to sleep, I went to my backyard with my written inventory and a book of matches. Standing quietly in my garden, one by one I burned the pages on which I had written my moral inventory. I could make out, in light generated by the flames, the names and words, people and situations that had shaped my life. Into the blackness, glowing, went the words: "I must always do things right or people will think I am stupid." "If I give people a chance, they will take advantage of me." "There is never enough to go around, so I better make sure I get mine first." "Always look like a nice guy or people won't like you." The pages dissolved into ash, floated downward, and were lost in the darkness.

When nothing remained to burn, I sat in the darkness reflecting on the undeniable fact that my efforts in working the Steps were slowly bringing about a dramatic shift in my personality. This process, so unscientific and non-rational, was producing significant changes. I was becoming more patient with others and with myself, slower to anger and more considerate of others' needs. Not all the time but more of the time. And not so they would like me but because acting toward others with consideration and courtesy seemed the natural thing to do. By becoming more gentle and forgiving toward myself, I could allow more of my authentic self to show in the world and work less to maintain a false self-image.

Because isolation is often a major dysfunctional and impoverishing feature of the addict's way of life, we cannot afford to maintain our condition of psychic withdrawal and secrecy. This is why we must involve another person in this venture of soul-searching, allowing them to enter with us into the dark recesses of our inner nature. We must relinquish the masks behind which we hide our secret, inner selves. *Isolation* does not mean we avoid social engagement, although that is often the case. It refers to psychic withdrawal, accompanied by erecting and maintaining a false self. Unfortunately, this destructive and well-conceived attempt to protect our ego from harm hinders our socialization and causes us to feel unworthy of a place in the human family. Recovery requires sharing our secrets with someone else.

The act of confession carries forward the process begun by acknowledging our character defects in Step Four. Telling another person our secrets allows us to soften and expiate the guilt we carry over past wrongdoings and furthers the healing of our shame—our sense of unworthiness as human beings.[7] We create the foundation on which we can build meaningful lives where there is the possibility of true intimacy.

Admitting to my sponsor that I harbored violent and destructive impulses and that I was sometimes jealous and envious of others required the courage and willingness to allow another person access to my shadow side. Throughout my Step work, I had been cultivating the qualities of courage and willingness, and now, sharing my secrets further expanded my capacity for humility and compassion. In the moment that I'd come forward and faced my fear of being seen as weak and flawed, I'd found strength and comfort in the discovery that I shared the human condition. I had begun cultivating the quality of humility that program literature forever reminds us is essential to our recovery.

In addition to describing past actions that harmed others, we reveal to our open-hearted listener the attitudes and motives that have shaped and guided our life, and that, we now begin to understand, are destructive to us. We speak of our unresolved resentments over things done to us over the years, acknowledging how often our mind is filled with criticisms and judgments, how frequently we burn with envy. Our honest and complete sharing furthers our recovery. The Twelve and Twelve puts it this way:

> . . . *Experience has taught us we cannot live alone with our pressing problems and the character defects which cause or aggravate them. If we have swept the searchlight of Step Four back and forth over our careers, and it has revealed in*

*stark relief those experiences we'd rather not remember, if we
have come to know how wrong thinking and action have
hurt us and others, then the need to quit living by ourselves
with those tormenting ghosts of yesterday gets more urgent
than ever. We have to talk to somebody about them.*[8]

In the days that followed taking my Fifth Step, I reflected
on the nature of sponsorship and its relationship to psychotherapy. The most obvious similarity is their mutual reliance on confession as an essential element for psychic
healing. Getting things off one's chest in the presence of a
non-judging person is clearly recognized as an important part
of the healing process in psychotherapy. Curiously, however, little is made of it in clinical training or in texts written
for therapists. While the literature stresses the need for the
clinician to listen and respond to the patient without convey-
ing his or her personal judgments, I was unable to find much
discussion of the healing power of confession itself. A significant exception was the following made by Jung in his book,
The Practice of Psychotherapy.

*The beginnings of psychoanalysis are in fact nothing else
than the scientific rediscovery of an ancient truth; even the
name that was given to the earliest method — catharsis, or
cleansing — is a familiar term in the classical rites of initia-
tion. . . . I must have a dark side too if I am to be whole;
and by becoming conscious of my shadow I remember once
more that I am a human being like any other. . . .
Through confession I throw myself into the arms of humanity again, freed at last from the burden of moral exile. The
goal of the cathartic method is full confession — not merely
the intellectual recognition of the facts with the head, but
their confirmation by the heart and the actual release of suppressed emotion.*[9]

Psychic healing is more than resolving the wounds of childhood. Sharing one's personal history and revealing one's

shadow to another person brings one back into the human family, signaling an end to isolation. Confession is not just telling someone about our sins and transgressions so he or she can advise us how to obtain absolution. Jung tells us confession and catharsis are more than the release of dammed up emotions; they involve the surrender of one's entire isolationist and defensive stance against humanity.

Recovery advances when a person reveals the dark secrets of the soul to another person capable of non-judgmental listening. It takes willingness on the part of the storyteller to tell the whole story, and it requires of the listener genuine acceptance and compassion. What life experiences allow the development of those healing attitudes in the listener? In training to become a counselor, I was exposed to methods for listening to others that were supposedly therapeutic. I always thought that these formulaic techniques were helpful in encouraging people to reveal the whole story.

But the kind of healing encounter we are talking about here demands more of the listener than listening skills; it requires his or her full engagement. It is not enough to act non-judgmentally in the face of what the other person reveals. One must, in fact, be capable of listening to whatever is shared with an open heart, sensing the shared humanity behind whatever motivations or actions the person describes. This ability cannot be taught in school or out of a book. It comes by the listener having experienced a similar confession; by the listener having faced the demons within him- or herself and shared with another what has been revealed; by the listener having been met with acceptance, understanding, and love.

As part of my preparation for becoming a psychotherapist, I underwent several years of therapy with a number of different therapists. Exploring one's psychic interior is essential to the professional development of those who choose this life work. I had to learn what behaviors in others aroused my impatience and critical judgments on the one hand, and my pity and over-identification on the other. This would help me remain present and balanced when my patients triggered those responses in me. It took years of experience practicing therapy and receiving consultation from other professionals to cultivate enough awareness to use, creatively rather than destructively, these feelings as they arose in the therapeutic relationship.

The challenge continues throughout a psychotherapist's professional life; discovering one's blind spots is an ongoing process of learning and growth. At the same time, undergoing one's own therapy provides a first-hand experience of how vulnerable one feels opening up his or her wounds and shadow side to another. Whether as a sponsor listening to a Fifth Step, or a therapist listening to a patient, nothing substitutes for having been there oneself, for learning reverence and respect for the vulnerability that revelation brings.

Transpersonal psychology speaks of the "wounded healer."[10] The Greek mythological figure Chiron is an archetypal expression of this concept. This *centaur* (half man and half horse)[11] was unintentionally wounded in the knee by a poison-tipped arrow shot by Heracles. Remorseful over what he had done, Heracles tended to the wound following Chiron's instructions, but the poison made the wound incurable. Because centaurs are immortal, Chiron carried forever a wound that would not heal. He became a great teacher of medical healing, and eventually Asclepius, the god of healing, came to learn from him the secrets of herbs and the power of snakes. Part of the wisdom that Chiron passed to Asclepius was the power of bringing one's own woundedness to the work of healing others.[12]

One of the great resources essential to psychic healing is the healer's contact with his or her own woundedness. A great danger in healing work, indeed in any helping activity, is the loss of awareness that the healer and person to be healed are in a shared predicament. Both must be in touch with the wounds they bear if the relationship is to serve as a vessel for change. If, for example, a psychotherapist perceives himself as beyond having his own psychological issues, he will fail to bring the necessary qualities of attention and compassion to his work. No matter how extensive his training or remarkable his intellectual capacities, if he fails to work out of the depths of his own humanness, his own suffering and struggles, he will not touch the places of pain and injury in the patient in ways that support whatever healing is possible.

For this touching to occur, the therapist/helper must have the capacity to empathize—to feel with and be moved by the patient. Willingness and the courage to remain open to one's own woundedness, and to touch another's pain and suffering with compassion and mercy, are necessary of all who wish to assist in the healing of others.

This capacity is an essential aspect of what Martin Buber calls the *I-Thou Relationship*. The other person is not seen as separate, as the one with problems. Rather, there is a sense that both the healer and the one being healed share the suffering, the grief common to all human beings; only the form and particular expression are unique. I am not suggesting that a therapist take on the client's problems as her own, nor that she express emotions that belong to the client to reveal. But I am saying that in those moments of a therapeutic relationship that are richest with potential for transformation, the therapist must be fully aware of her own woundedness, while inviting the client to open fully to his or her own. The same may be said of one seeking to help another along the path of recovery through listening to his or her Fifth Step.

Again, using my experiences as a therapist, I wanted to explore aspects of the healing relationship to better understand what happens when one reads an inventory to someone who has already read his or her inventory to another. I am reminded of the difference between those clinical hours during which the patient plays the role of sick one while I play helpful therapist and those remarkable moments when we are two beings in an encounter that transcends our separateness. In those special and all too rare moments, whatever issues are facing the client, whatever emotion is being released, there is a sense that we are both being healed by a love that is, at the same time, within both of us and beyond us. We lose that otherwise persistent sense of isolation and separation. Most of the time, the client and I spend our time somewhere in between those two extremes. Important work takes place here, but the profound healing possible for both of us awaits those special times.

Sharing my Fourth Step with my sponsor was truly a healing event. And what made it so was the fact that he listened out of the depths of his own experience in recovery and personal transformation, not as an expert or as my superior. He approached the task willing to listen to me with an open heart because others had listened to him in that way. He was aware of his own humanness as he listened to my efforts to describe honestly my shadow parts and share stories of things I had done that still hung like heavy chains around my neck. Listening as he did, my sponsor helped me take another step out of the hell of compulsive living toward liberation; he helped me move from self-loathing toward self-acceptance. At the same time, he taught me, by his example, the importance of bringing my own woundedness into my work with others. He reminded me that all of my training and skill development could not substitute for the greatest resource I had available—my own humanity, the fact that I was also just another recovering person.

It is not easy for man so to change himself . . . it is one of the most tragic facts about ourselves that we have always imagined that it was easy, but of no great profit, to change one's own nature, and hard, but immensely valuable, to change outer nature.

— Gerald Heard

Healing involves more than contemplation. It advances through action taken to get things right, deeds that follow the guidance of what we call conscience . . . what reestablishes wholeness are the actions that spring from the voices within that the ancients called their gods.

— Arthur Egendorf

Willingness is a form of open-heartedness. There are rocks which have been resting on the ocean floor for millions of years. They are still dry inside. If our hearts are closed we will not be able to find the teachings. We must be willing to give up attachment and grasping. Bees feed on the nectar of flowers; they do not cling to the blossoms.

— Tarthang Tulku

CHAPTER SIX

Willingness And Self-Forgiveness

*Were entirely ready to have God remove all these defects of character.**

The Big Book devotes to Step Six only one short paragraph, which concludes by asking: "Are we now ready to let God remove from us all the things which we have admitted are objectionable? Can He now take them all—every one?" It also suggests that, "if we still cling to something we will not let go, we ask God to help us be willing."[1] These questions invite us to examine the extent of our readiness to live without dependence on those character attitudes and beliefs that have served to protect and reinforce the illusion of the supremacy of the ego. To answer them honestly in the affirmative requires we do a fair amount of soul-searching and preparation.

When I first approached this Step, it seemed like a quiet resting place granted those who have made the Herculean effort necessary to complete Steps Four and Five. After writing my moral inventory and reading it to my sponsor, I thought

---

* Step Six, the Twelve Steps of Overeaters Anonymous, adapted from the Twelve Steps of Alcoholics Anonymous. The complete Twelve Steps of AA appear on page 221.

it would be easy to reflect on how nice life would be without those pernicious thoughts. What fool would be unwilling to surrender thoughts and attitudes that obviously caused so much pain and unhappiness? Who would not want to be free of resentment, guilt, and fear—those feelings that prevent us from living more freely and joyfully in each unfolding moment?

At first, I thought this Step only required that I demonstrate sufficient desire to bring God to remove the negative aspects of my personality, whereby they would be replaced with positive ones. Who could pass up the chance for a complete personality overhaul and the opportunity to be an ideal loving, honest, and kind person? An easy path to sainthood. I was skeptical that such a profound personality change could occur simply by telling my Higher Power I was willing to have my character defects removed and then readying myself for it. But since that was how I understood the Step and given the fact that I wanted to be a nicer, happier person, I expressed to my Higher Power that I was ready. Then, quickly, I moved on to the Seventh Step, hoping to find some suggestions that were a bit more substantial than I found in Step Six.

At about this time I happened to attend an OA weekend retreat. About one hundred people gathered on the grounds of a beautiful ecumenical retreat center to listen to and share experiences as compulsive overeaters recovering through working the Twelve Steps. Months earlier, I had heard a tape recording of a very funny talk given by the man who was to be the retreat leader. I came to the retreat hoping to hear more from him and to share in the humor that often marks OA gatherings. The retreat began on Friday evening with the leader telling his story, which began with years of bingeing and obesity before coming to OA. He then spoke with gratitude about coming to OA, becoming abstinent and losing over two hundred pounds through the support of the fellowship and working the Twelve Steps. He concluded with a description of some of the physical, emotional, and spiritual changes brought about through his active engagement with OA and the Twelve Steps.

While I was impressed with how much his life had been affected by coming to OA, I was somewhat put off when he attributed his professional success to daily conversations with his Higher Power. He seemed to be suggesting that, because he was willing to talk to his God every morning, his God made sure jobs would come his way when he needed money. I was hearing the message I had heard so often in other Twelve Step meetings: if you have faith in God, He will influence events so that you will not suffer. I was uncomfortable with this, but my displeasure was overshadowed by my enjoyment at hearing his humor and seeing his obvious good nature and love for the people in the room.

When he finished his story, he invited people to come to the podium to share their thoughts and feelings with the group. Some spoke of their excitement about being at the retreat and their hope that it would prove a positive experience. Others expressed trepidation about what might happen to them during the weekend. Among the latter group of speakers were people who said they feared being left out by the group. Many had not allowed themselves to participate in a group experience for years. They felt vulnerable and frightened. A few of the speakers took the opportunity to relate some of their history before coming to OA. One or two speakers told of struggles they were having in their lives, describing painful losses and feelings of confusion and despair. All spoke in one way or another about years of having struggled with overeating and weight problems and how hopeless they felt before coming to the program.

The atmosphere of warmth and acceptance was helping to bring down the walls of fear that kept us in our customary fortresses of isolation. As each person spoke and was met by the group's interest and acceptance, we ceased being a collection of strangers and became a community. By the end of the evening I felt very warm toward a number of people. When the session formally ended I stayed and talked. I had a wonderful time getting to know people and sharing laughs and hugs.

I should point out that before coming to OA, I would never have stayed in the room once the session had ended. Whenever I attended workshops or retreats in the past, I invariably left immediately. Sometimes I would go for a solitary walk; other times I would return to my room to write in my journal or meditate. I had always told myself that I did these things to be able to reflect on what was said during the meeting. But by this time in my recovery I knew myself better. I understood I was a person who tended to isolate. I was, despite my outer appearance as a friendly, self-confident person, rather shy and fearful of others. Nevertheless, this evening I chose to remain, despite some anxiety, and engaged in friendly conversation. When I finally crawled into bed that night, I looked forward to the remainder of the retreat with eager anticipation.

The following morning, we gathered to hear the leader share his understanding and experiences with the first three Steps. He spoke of how he had admitted his powerlessness over food, came to believe a Power greater than himself could help, and made a decision to turn his will and life over to the care of his Higher Power. I enjoyed his candor and warmth. He was extremely funny and had us all laughing throughout his presentation. By the time we broke for lunch, I was in great spirits; during the meal, I engaged in lively conversation with the men and women at my table. We swapped stories about our old bingeing days and about how our lives had been changed by the program.

In the afternoon session, the leader spoke about his experiences with Steps Four, Five, and Six. He described the format he used to write his moral inventory and told us how he gave his inventory to his sponsor. He told us how he got down on his knees and prayed to God to remove his character defects, explaining that he had maintained his personal relationship with his God ever since that time through morning conversations. God was, for him, a friend from whom he received guidance each day. He believed that God would take care of all his problems so long as he continued to pray every day and ask for guidance.

As he spoke about his personal relationship with God, I began to experience irritation. My mind began filling with judgments, and it became increasingly difficult for me to listen to him. Finally, I tuned out his words and began attending to what was going through my mind. For some reason, I was enraged by what appeared to be some kind of feudal theory of man's relationship to God. I had long ago rejected the notion of God as a mythical, kind and loving feudal lord, where human beings were either devoted servants and serfs or wayward roving peasants. Those of God's servants who faithfully till His fields and willingly turn over the harvest are blessed by the Lord and given sufficient food and shelter. *What a load of bull*, I thought. *How could a grown person believe such nonsense?*

Feeling irritated, I turned my attention back to the speaker. He was describing how wonderful his life had become since turning his will and life over to God. He told several stories of good fortune and success in his personal and professional life, which he attributed to his daily conversations with God. Finally, he concluded his talk by underscoring the heart of his message—God takes care of those who believe in Him and try to carry out His will. He offered his belief that this is the message of Twelve Step recovery programs. Faith is necessary—faith that if one turns over his or her life to God and takes the Twelve Steps, God will provide for that individual. God will not only remove the urge to compulsively overeat but also provide divine assistance when necessary.

By the time he had finished talking about Step Six, I was in some dark tunnel, alone. As individuals began going up to the podium to share their experiences with this Step, I felt estranged from everyone in the room. I felt as though I was listening and observing from a psychic isolation booth. I sat in stoney silence as men and women shared their experiences. I listened as others spoke more generally about their understanding of and relationship with their Higher Power, feeling a mixture of boredom and annoyance. I began wishing the retreat was over so I could pack my things and go home.

My sponsor, who had been sitting beside me, noticed that something was disturbing me. Not realizing the nature or extent of my distress, he nudged me and suggested I go to the podium and share what was on my mind. I shook my head; I didn't want to speak to anyone, let alone to a whole roomful of people. As far as I could tell, I had nothing to say; I just wanted to be left alone. He said I looked as though I needed to talk about whatever was going on. I could have sworn that no part of me wanted to address the group, and yet suddenly I watched my hand go up. My mind screamed at me to put my hand down. I had no idea what I was going to say or why I had raised my hand in the first place. Despite the fact that a number of people were waving their hands toward the leader, he turned toward me and invited me to the podium.

As I walked to the front of the room, I still had no idea what I was going to say. Maybe I would just stand there staring at the group, looking and feeling embarrassed. As I turned to face the group, I was suddenly swept by a rising flood of rage. Looking out at the faces of the men and women I had been getting to know during the retreat, I could not find one that was familiar. I thought they were all stupid fools. How could they honestly believe the sorts of things being said by the leader? I wanted to shock them. I began to speak. More accurately, words began pouring from my mouth. I said, in a loud, angry voice, that I wasn't about to give up all of the defenses I had developed over a lifetime to protect me against a cruel and unfriendly world. The world was a dangerous place; anyone could see that. When it came right down to the wire, there was no one to trust but yourself. A person would be a fool to trust in some fictional Supreme Being.

As I stood silently in the aftermath of my initial comments, I began remembering incidents during my childhood. I recalled, as a young Jewish boy, listening to my parents speak with rage and horror about the Holocaust. As information about the nature and extent of the Nazi atrocities appeared in the American press, it became a constant topic of discussion. I remembered quite clearly thinking to myself on one of those occasions that there could be no God if such a thing could happen. Again becoming conscious of the sea of faces staring at me, I said that I could never believe in a God who could have abandoned the six million Jewish people exterminated in Hitler's death camps. Where the hell was "Mr. Good-friend" then? And where was this God when so many of the other awful things happened to decent people who held on to their faith in Him only to suffer intolerable hardships and suffering?

A voice went off in my head as I stood in front of the stunned group. *Just what the hell are you doing? You are wrecking the weekend for everyone. Why don't you just stop talking and take your seat before you make things worse?* But before I had time to consider leaving the podium, I explained angrily that, when, as a young boy, I heard of the fate of six million of my fellow Jews at the hands of the Nazis, it had destroyed my capacity for faith in a loving God. No such God, capable of affecting the affairs of human beings, could possibly exist without taking some protective action to help the faithful. What did God do for those who must have prayed to Him as they were taken from their homes, transported in cattle cars, and exterminated in various ways in the concentration camps?

I explained that the leader's model of God and spirituality had been a central force in driving me away from religion. I couldn't understand how intelligent adults, or children either, could believe that the events in the Bible actually happened through divine intervention, or that a Supreme Being ruled the universe and chose the Jewish people or anyone else to carry out its intentions on earth. I told the group that as much as I had wanted a new bicycle for Hanukkah as a youngster, I steadfastly refused to pray to God to help me get one. When I was thirteen and my grandfather lay seriously ill in a hospital bed after a heart attack, I refused to pray for his recovery. And when he did recover, I took satisfaction in the fact that his return to health could in no way be attributed to my having prayed to God for assistance.

I stopped speaking, realizing that something had shifted within me. My willingness to openly express my rage and doubt had shaken loose some encrusted skepticism. I was beginning to sense an opening within me—I was experiencing the touch of my Higher Power. *Touch* isn't the right word, but no other is better. It was as though a door had opened and a fresh, clear wind was blowing across my face. I felt peaceful.

My awareness returned to the room and the people sitting before me. I realized that, just as acknowledging powerlessness over my eating compulsion made room for me to seek the help of a Higher Power, admitting fully my skepticism and doubt allowed me to experience a spiritual awakening. Through my public, spontaneous expression, I had revealed and released the anguish and fear of that little boy who had so long ago listened repeatedly to the cries of rage and terror from his parents over the plight of the Jewish people at the hands of the Nazis. I recalled the frequent, horrible nightmares of being separated from my parents and locked up alone in a concentration camp. I sensed the terror still held in that child-place within me and at the same moment felt it begin melting. And my anger at the God whom I believed could and should have protected those suffering men, women, and children no longer prevented me from feeling my thirst and hunger for an experience of the sacred within my psyche. Then I thanked people for their willingness to let me express myself and returned to my seat.

As I sat down, my sponsor smiled and took my arm. Leaning toward me, he laughed quietly and said, "Well, Phillip,

I had no idea what was going on with you, but I sure am glad you got up there and said what was on your mind. I really love you."

"Thanks," I replied, "I really love you too. And thanks for the push."

During the remainder of the weekend, I had several moving conversations with people who had been struggling with particular issues preventing them from exploring the possibility of encountering a Higher Power within. Several men and women shared their inner torments and constricting doubts. A number of them spoke about the slow but powerful changes that began to take place within them as a result of hearing me share my struggles. The leader continued to share his experiences in recovery. And while I listened and enjoyed his stories and insights, I knew I had gotten what I had come for. At the end of the retreat, I returned home with new insights into the power and significance of Step Six. I understood what it meant to become entirely ready to have God remove my character defects, to move further into a relationship with my inner spiritual nature.

In the days that followed the retreat I thought more about this Step. I realized that so long as I had held a secret rage against God and mankind, I could not open myself to a spiritual experience. No philosophical arguments, no miracles, and no religious practices had achieved what my public expression had accomplished. My public outcry reflected my willingness to honor my doubt and to offer it up as a form of prayer. I no longer viewed this Step and the one that followed as a quick slide between the hard work of Steps Four and Five on one side and Eight and Nine on the other. Rather, I saw that in combination with Step Seven, it involved a profound shift in consciousness requiring my willingness to forgo the old protective devices I'd erected over a lifetime to protect myself from emotional harm.

It is a natural tendency for us as human beings to guard and protect our self-images and egos. By committing ourselves to acting in ways contrary to that tendency, we enter a new stage of maturity and moral development. Slowly, we grow free of what the poet Robert Bly calls "the long bag we drag behind us"; we become less driven to respond in automatic and obsolete ways to the people and events in our present life.[2]

Step Six is a further commitment to putting our faith and trust in the power and wisdom of our Higher Self. It enables us to abandon the old defenses and automatic reactions developed in childhood to protect us from overpowering emotions such as shame, fear of abandonment, and our own natural rage.

A paradox exists at the heart of Step Six. To the extent we are willing to relinquish control over our character defects, we open to the possibility of altering them. Over the years I have practiced psychotherapy, I have been reminded again and again that this paradox is at the heart of all therapeutic change. Changing aspects of ourselves begins with acceptance of ourselves as we are. Willingness involves openness, acceptance of what is a welcoming of what could be. The literature of Alcoholics Anonymous does not offer specific suggestions for the removal of our character defects. Rather than trying to will or force this process, we are reminded by Step Six that we must become willing to invite the healing force of our Higher Power to assist in their removal. Just as we discovered that we could not force ourselves to stop behaving compulsively through willpower, we now realize that we cannot discharge our character defects by trying to crush them as though they were enemies.

In the Christian tradition from which the Twelve Steps are drawn, a person prays that God show His mercy and remove the barriers between him- or herself and the Divine. Character defects tend to be viewed as "sinful" thoughts and actions that in themselves are barriers preventing human contact with God. Human beings may be seen as defective by nature, their only hope of salvation lying in God's willingness to remove their spiritual blemishes.

From this viewpoint, only if God takes mercy on us do we become worthy of joining Him in heaven. This is perhaps the most prevalent Christian interpretation of the term grace. This is not the only way to understand this important concept.

A number of definitions for the word *grace* can be found in the *Random House Dictionary of the English Language*. Of several that are theological in nature, two are relevant to our discussion. The first, which reflects Christian doctrine, defines *grace* as "the freely given, unmerited favor and love of God." This definition implies a state of being over which a person has no control, a state of divine bliss. Some theologians following this approach suggest that humans are always in a state of grace. It is our character defects that prevent us from experiencing the joy of this state.

On the other extreme is the more fundamentalist approach to the concept of original sin. Viewing human beings as having literally fallen from God's grace, those who espouse this view consider human beings utterly unworthy of God's favor. Since we are all unworthy sinners, we can only work and sacrifice for God, without any real hope or expectation of redemption. Our hope is that He might take pity on us in our suffering and grant us grace solely out of his mercy.

A second theological meaning offered by the dictionary defines *grace* as "the influence or spirit of God operating in man to regenerate or strengthen him." This definition suggests that grace is a quality or capacity *within* human beings, rather than a state or gift given by God. If we are capable of experiencing grace as a quality in the human heart, then we can, if we wish, take steps to cultivate it. One way to do so is to relate to adversity as a vehicle for expanding our capacity to experience the spirit of God within us. While we do not actively seek pain and hardship, when it does come our way we can use the experience to develop those resources and qualities that express the spiritual power in ourselves. To the extent that we are capable of perceiving hardship as a teacher rather than a personal affront committed against us, we grow emotionally and spiritually.

Moving forward with Step Six, we attempt to face openly the pain and hardship of human experience. We stop seeking ways of avoiding and denying the difficulties of life. We practice living more fully, opening ourselves to the changing flow of existence, taking every opportunity to embrace the full range of human experience. Nothing is avoided, not even the many times life is too much for us and we resort to our old defenses. We make room for all of it—bringing everything into the light of awareness and self-acceptance. This is how spiritual and psychological transformation and healing occur; this is the way to wholeness, not through rejection, but through acceptance and integration. Arthur Egendorf suggests psychic healing is only possible when we stop battling:

> *Healing is inclusive, whereas whatever we battle against we exclude and despise. And so from a healing perspective, it is self-defeating to try to reject what we see as unworthy or threatening in ourselves or others. Healing occurs as we develop the openness, care and vision to cast in a worthy light whatever appears before us.*[3]

Everyday frustrations can become our spiritual teachers, reminding us where we cling to our fixed notions of how things should be. Even major crises and personal losses can serve as powerful vehicles with which we can soften and transform our character defects. Let me give you an example.

Many years ago, in my early thirties, I took up the martial art of Aikido. Almost at once it became a passion with me. My wife and I went to class daily and sometimes twice a day out of love and dedication to our training. We loved the intensity of the classes, the physical contact, the demands it put on our bodies and minds. For more than three years it played a major role in our lives. We built our social lives and our work schedules around our training program. In fact, my master's thesis for graduate school was on the use of martial art training as a tool for psychological growth.

Having moved through the lower ranks, the time came for me to prepare for my black belt examination. One morning during that period I took a routine fall and dislocated my knee. While it healed sufficiently for most purposes after about a month's rest, whenever I tried to train, it would begin to bother me. In addition, I began having trouble with my back, occasionally throwing it out, forcing me to stop training for several weeks each time. For a period of several months I experienced injury after injury. Finally, I came to the conclusion that my body could no longer tolerate the pounding and twisting to which I was subjecting it and gave up my training. Because it would have meant our being apart night after night, my wife also stopped training. It was a great loss for both of us, and even after many years we spoke occasionally of what it might be like to train again. Of course, we never thought seriously that we might return to Aikido training. But then an Aikido dojo, a training school, opened near our home.

At first we decided to take a few classes just to check things out. But immediately, we wanted to train regularly and started attending classes often. Without taking into account that I was many years older than when I had trained before and that I had once suffered several serious injuries, I rushed into training intensely and attempted things for which my body was unprepared. One evening I twisted my knee rather seriously and several weeks later severely injured my back. I stopped going to classes for a while, wondering whether I would be able to ever train seriously again.

In the meantime my wife continued to train. Missing our times together and the fun we had practicing techniques on the mat and at home, I soon became depressed and resentful. I spoke to my sponsor about the situation, and he suggested working my program around it. He advised me to start by examining which parts of my situation I was powerless over and which I might be able to change. Then, he continued, I could develop an inventory of resources and possible courses of action should I attempt to continue training. And, if training in Aikido was not going to be possible, I could pray and meditate for the strength and inner guidance needed to face the loss.

Following my sponsor's suggestions, I decided to do something that I had not done when I first got injured years earlier—I went for help. This time I saw a doctor who referred me to a physical therapist, who, in turn, helped me strengthen and stretch the problem areas. Soon I was able to begin training again. This time, under the watchful eye of my teacher, I trained with greater attention and concentrated on what I needed to do to protect myself from further injury. I had to acknowledge my physical limitations and practice within them.

At the same time, I continued investigating various methods of healing and correcting my physical disability and eventually found a Yoga teacher who thought he could help me. He designed a program of Yoga therapy for me, and each morning and evening I would do the series of movements he prescribed.

Slowly, I've developed the strength and flexibility in my legs and spine to train more actively so long as I maintain some awareness of what I must do to protect my back. Every once in a while I overdo things and the next morning I feel sore and stiff. I accept that I cannot train as hard as I once did, but staying within my physical limitations I can have lots of fun and can advance my practice. A week before my forty-eighth birthday, I took and passed my black belt examination.

Working the program around this experience required looking at how much I held on to having things be the way I wanted them to be. Looking honestly and compassionately at the suffering caused by my unwillingness to face the truth about my situation allowed me to recognize my resentment toward my wife for being able to train injury-free. I saw that self-pity and bitterness came more easily than committing myself to a serious rehabilitation program that required effort, time, and money.

Through both my Yoga practice and Aikido training, I rediscovered how impatient I could be. I wanted the Yoga therapy to bring strength and flexibility at once; I wanted to improve in Aikido more quickly than I was able. However, working the Steps, in particular Step Six, I was able to work with all of these thoughts and feelings. As a result, I have come to a place of peace and balance regarding Aikido. I don't train as often as I might like, but I accept the reality of things. I sometimes feel jealous when I see my wife advancing more quickly, and I am able to watch the jealousy without feeling compelled to act on it or even carry tension over it. On those occasional mornings when I wake up stiff and sore, I remind myself that I might need to ease up for the next few days rather than pushing myself and complaining about my discomfort. But there are days when I push and mornings when complaining is all I seem able to do. And that's all right, too, because I'm still growing and learning.

Step Six, with its emphasis on willingness, implies that we must be gentle and patient with ourselves. Bringing those qualities to our efforts allows us to expose our character defects to the light of non-judgmental awareness. When we are free to observe, without reaction, the surfacing of traces of egocentricity, we are able to choose actions that heal. For instance, when I felt impatient because my back was not getting better as fast as I wanted and I merely noticed the appearance of that impatience, I could choose acceptance and gratitude. As a result, my impatience did not generate frustration, bitterness, and self-pity. Rather, seeing my impatience as a character defect, I was able to bring those healing qualities to my situation. I did not have to deny or suppress my impatience. By acknowledging and working with my impatience, I was able to transform it. With regard to my Aikido injury, working both on the physical level with the injury and on the spiritual level with my character defects, true healing took place.

The process of working with character defects is similar to the way I can approach temptations to eat compulsively. Working with the desire to eat compulsively is my basic spiritual practice; no matter how far along I am in recovery, I always return to it as the foundation of my new way of life. It is somewhat like meditation practice, where we use a centering device (we will examine this more fully in our discussion of Step Eleven). In meditation it can be a word, the movement of the breath, the ever-changing flow of sensation, thought, and feeling, or whatever provides a point of focus for the mind. When the mind wanders, we gently bring our attention back to the device and lightly hold it there. Over time we find it easier to stay focused on the object of attention, and as we continue to work with the meditation practice, we find that we remain focused more and more of the time. When we discover that we have lost our way, we are able with much more lightness and ease to bring ourselves back.

My capacity to move through the day without using food other than as fuel for the body is my centering device. When urges to compulsively eat arise, I investigate these "tempter thoughts" and discover a world of inner experiences surrounding them. Sometimes I discover feelings such as boredom, irritation, and loneliness. Becoming aware of them gives me the opportunity to experience them and decide whether some action might be appropriate or whether I need only to allow them space within my consciousness. Whatever course of action I choose to take in light of my emotions, I have chosen not to eat over them. I am developing, not willpower, which has never helped me to stop compulsively eating, but awareness and freedom of choice. *This is the abstinence the program promises.*

I am now able to put space between the urgings of the tempter and the act of putting food into my mouth. I am being restored to sanity with regard to my eating. When the impulse to act from my character defects arises, in the same way, I find that I am no longer compelled to act automatically in response to its directive. I am developing the capacity to choose to act independently of my compulsion to eat and my impulses to act from my egocentricity.

Recovery is growing in the capacity to choose, and this capacity is what marks the mature human being. The Sixth Step is a commitment to our own maturation process; our willingness to let go of the defenses that protect our egocentricity marks our readiness to grow up and face the challenges of adulthood. And having reached that state of readiness, we are prepared to take further action to reduce the power of our character defects to shape and determine our feelings and behavior.

*What we strive for in the effort to resolve the tension be-
tween our sense of inferiority and our grandiosity is not
modesty but humility—spiritual dignity.*

— *Jean Hardy*

*The harder we try with the conscious will to do some-
thing, the less we shall succeed. Proficiency and the
results of proficiency come only to those who have
learned the paradoxical art of simultaneously doing and
not doing, of combining relaxation with activity, of letting go as a person in order that the immanent and transcendent Unknown Quantity may take hold.*

— *Aldous Huxley*

*It is not so much a matter of God's "knowing" our short-
comings and putting up with us: rather, it is man who
must know his own shortcomings and call on the Spirit
we call God to give man the ability to improve and the
vision to see his abilities and defects realistically.*

— *Harold Kushner*

*Embrace all that you most fear or find repugnant, the
better to realize that everything in the Universe, being
inseparably related, is therefore holy.*

— *Lama Marpa's instruction to Malarepa*

CHAPTER SEVEN

Humbly Asking

Humbly asked Him to remove our shortcomings. *

In its brief discussion of Step Seven, the Big Book advises: once Step Six has been completed, a simple prayer is to be recited, which reads as follows:

> *My Creator, I am now willing that you should have all of me, good and bad. I pray that you now remove from me every single defect of character which stands in the way of my usefulness to you and my fellows. Grant me strength, as I go out from here, to do your bidding. Amen.*[1]

The subject is closed with the comment, "We have then completed *Step Seven.*" *That's it?* I thought on first reflection. *Just a little prayer asking God to remove all traces of my egocentricity I had painstakingly identified? There has to be more to this Step than just reciting a prayer. Further research is definitely in order.* I turned to the chapter devoted to Step Seven in the Twelve and Twelve and, at first, found little that was helpful. The discussion centered around the concept of humility and concluded with the following suggestion:

---

* Step Seven, the Twelve Steps of Overeaters Anonymous, adapted from the Twelve Steps of Alcoholics Anonymous. The complete Twelve Steps of AA appears on page 221.

> We now ought to be willing to try humility in seeking the removal of our other shortcomings just as we did when we admitted that we were powerless over alcohol, and came to believe that a Power greater than ourselves could restore us to sanity. If that degree of humility could enable us to find the grace by which such a deadly obsession could be banished, then there must be hope of the same result respecting any other problem we could possibly have.[2]

Humility had always been associated in my mind with humiliation and shame. Childhood memories of parental ridicule and manipulation through shame surfaced, and I realized why I had such strong resistance to the suggestion that I cultivate humility. Endeavoring to become or to acknowledge myself as small and weak was out of the question. Hadn't my vulnerability with and dependence on my parents been a source of tremendous pain and anger? I saw now that this Step, like many of the previous ones, required facing unpleasant memories and emotions. Once again I would have to encounter feelings I'd carefully hidden from the world behind my inflated ego, feelings I'd blotted out of consciousness through compulsive overeating. In addition, being required to face feelings of dependency and incompleteness, I had to surrender once more to the idea that consciousness cannot be changed through willful efforts alone.

A theme that recurs throughout program literature is that we can take action and apply great effort to the tasks of recovery, but deep psychic changes come about outside our conscious control. In order to work Step Seven, I must bring my will to the task of acting in new ways, while at the same time recognizing that whatever psychic changes occur are up to my Higher Power.

Once more I had to remind myself that the process of recovery has both active and yielding aspects. In this context, I could see that humility is an expression of the human capacity to surrender, to yield, to a Power greater than oneself.[3] We must cultivate the willingness to work tirelessly to transform our character defects, while understanding that the extent and speed with which they change is beyond our control. Whatever efforts we make must be undertaken in this spirit, or we risk the danger of carrying out our spiritual work, not in the service of our Higher Power but merely to shore up our egocentricity.

Spiritual materialism is always a danger because so much of our thinking has been egocentric; we must be watchful of the tendency of the ego-mind to use spiritual work to enhance itself rather than relinquish its control to the Higher Self.[4] We must be careful not to confuse humility with self-depreciation. The latter is merely another character defect masquerading as a spiritual quality, a form of grandiosity in disguise. Any perception of ourselves as inferior to others is an expression of egocentricity. It is no better or worse than believing ourselves superior to others. In recovery, we learn to recognize our unique strengths and weaknesses without using them to either inflate or diminish our sense of worth. Rather than rate ourselves or others, we cultivate self-respect and self-esteem through relinquishing our *identification* with the ego. This is how we practice true humility, a humility that grows as we rely more and more on the power and wisdom of our Higher Self within.

While I realized that Step Seven required that I surrender my character defects to my Higher Power, I still wanted to know what actions I might take to help the process along. I turned to my Step sponsor for direction, but when he offered his suggestions, I balked in my typical fashion. Explaining that he recited the Seventh Step Prayer every morning upon rising and that it had helped him foster the appropriate attitude of humility, he recommended that I try it. I was still uncomfortable about prayers; I was still holding on to the belief that change came only through my own efforts, and I was associating praying with soliciting the aid of some outside power. Clearly, humility was exactly what I lacked, and part of my mind exploited my vulnerability by harping on how stupid and weak-willed I would become were I to do what my sponsor suggested.

Nevertheless, I knew that if I hoped to move forward in my recovery, I must become willing to do whatever it would take to execute this Step. So I began praying for the removal of my character defects every morning during a period of silent prayer and meditation. I began each morning session with the Seventh Step Prayer, reminding myself that whatever changes were going to come about in my character defects would come through the power of my Higher Self, rather than through my conscious effort.

In addition, I returned to reading spiritual literature, looking for guidance on what other actions might further my efforts to transform my character defects. I was comforted by the consistent reminder that the goal of spiritual work is wholeness and psychic integration, rather than the destruction of the ego or any other aspect of the psyche. The readings I was drawn to reiterated that my ego was not to be destroyed, only placed in the service of my Higher Self. I was advised to cultivate my unique qualities and talents in order to express my full human potential, and to use them in service to others rather than to inflate my own sense of importance.

One of the fundamental psychological principles on which the Twelve Step process, as I understand it, rests is the idea that emotions and behaviors are expressions of thoughts and attitudes. As we have seen, particularly in our examination of character defects, how and what we think dictates how we respond to events and people. The message of the Big Book is that the path to altering our automatic emotional and behavioral reactions is through changing how we think—changing our beliefs and attitudes. This principle is not unique to AA. It can be found not only at the basis of many of the religious traditions we have been discussing, but also throughout the works of the major Greek philosophers whose ideas shaped much of Western philosophy.[5] These thinkers all expressed the belief that thoughts and attitudes are an important element in the formation of *passions* such as anger, fear, and grief and that one's *passions*, in turn, could be modified by changing one's thoughts and attitudes.

Several modern schools of psychology and psychotherapy also take this idea as the theoretical basis for their work. Most notable is Albert Ellis's Rational-Emotive Therapy. Ellis has built his entire model of psychotherapy on the idea that people who suffer from emotional difficulties are plagued by what he calls "irrational thinking." By this he means that they carry assumptions about themselves, other people, and reality that perpetuate unnecessary, unpleasant feelings. We can, Ellis believes, relieve much of our suffering through careful re-examination of these noxious assumptions and, consequently, through our efforts to counter them.

Ellis and most of his followers do not consider unconscious attitudes, memories, and emotions that are not immediately accessible to awareness to be significant. I believe that Ellis's approach suffers because he discounts the importance of the unconscious as a source of motivation. A former client, who drove a cab for a living, comes to mind. Whenever he turned a corner and saw another cab pick up a fare, he would punish himself mercilessly for having failed to come down that particular street earlier. For years, he had been making himself depressed and severely harmed his already fragile self-esteem by demanding of himself the capacity of precognition. In part, it was the assumption that he could somehow know beforehand that a fare was waiting on a particular street that produced his suffering. And yet my attempts to help him to simply stop thinking in the way he had did not produce change. Until he and I identified what had been heretofore *unconscious* attitudes and beliefs that supported his "irrational belief," he continued to expect things of himself that were clearly impossible.

Something more is required than simply applying reason and logic to irrational beliefs, something powerful enough to cause a shift at the deeper levels of the psyche. Why is that so?

Let's try an experiment that may help answer that question. Notice your breath for a moment. Without trying to change the pattern, be aware of whether you release all of the air in your lungs as you exhale. Most of us retain large quantities of air, thereby restricting the ability of the lungs to function fully and properly. Constricted breathing results in less oxygen being fed to the blood and less carbon dioxide being removed. Or, perhaps as you do this experiment, you discover that you hold your chest or belly tight on the inspiration so that only a limited amount of oxygen can be drawn into the lungs. Restriction of the inhalation also adversely affects the ability of your lungs to do their job.

Let's assume that, having identified one of these patterns during the experiment, you decide that you want to change the way you breathe to ensure better oxygen/carbon dioxide exchange. Committing yourself to a program of better breathing, you could start by observing your breath, making sure to fill your lungs on the inspiration and forcing out the air on the exhalation. So far, so good. But then what happens? Within a minute or two you invariably forget to concentrate, and as soon as your attention lapses your old breathing pattern returns.

We can alter the fullness of a few breaths through various forms of body therapies designed to help us release tension. We can also alter the holding patterns that restrict the natural functioning of our muscles involved in breathing. But our attempts to practice fuller breathing through awareness and conscious will are doomed to fail. The reason is obvious: to the extent that it is an unconscious process, breathing is directed by forces outside of our awareness. Because it is also subject to conscious control, we can influence it for short periods of time. But sooner or later, we will forget about our breathing because our attention is needed elsewhere, and when we do, the unconscious patterns reassert themselves.

Similarly, attempting to alter our unconscious thought and belief patterns simply by trying to attend to and modify their expression is a hopeless undertaking. For a brief period we might remain aware of our thinking, and for that time we would be capable of acting independently of the automatic motivating thoughts. Take, as an example, the impulse to scratch. Usually, when we feel a mild itch, it does not even reach conscious awareness before we bring our hand to scratch it. But if we make a conscious effort, we can, for a short time, bring enough attention to our impulses to notice the itch and the impulse to scratch without acting on that impulse. Most of the time, however, we cannot maintain continuous awareness; we lapse into unconsciousness regarding our responses to familiar discomforts, and this is where we remain most of the time.

While the discovery that our thoughts influence our emotions and actions might be an important one, usually just this, along with the attempt to consciously change our thoughts, cannot produce lasting changes. If our character defects are to be altered, work must be done at the deeper level of the unconscious. Some of this work we can do by conscious will, but much is directed by forces our ego-minds cannot control—what I've been calling the *Higher Self*. This is where spiritual work is necessary. What, then, do I mean by a spiritual approach to reducing the harmful effects of one's character defects?

As I'd already discovered, one important step I could take toward modifying my obsolete, unconscious thoughts and attitudes involved letting go of the unhelpful attitude that they are bad and sinful. Carving up the world into things I label as *good* and *bad* perpetuates the very belief system I am seeking to transcend. This dualistic thinking inevitably leads to engaging in fruitless struggles with myself as I attempt to make changes through my conscious will, an effort I had come to believe was doomed to failure.

I began by trying to maintain an attitude of self-forgiveness and loving kindness for myself. I reminded myself that just as I was powerless over my food compulsion, I have been powerless over the forces of egocentricity that had dominated my life. I brought whatever gentleness and compassion I could find within me as I moved along this path, particularly as I took steps to reduce the influence of my egocentric mind. Fortified with these healing attitudes, I was ready to move forward.

The Twelve and Twelve is emphatic about the need to continually investigate the attitudes and emotions that rise within us when we experience a situation as unpleasant. "It is a spiritual axiom that every time we are disturbed, no matter what the cause, there is something wrong *with us*."[6] Here, we are being given the key to what willful action we can take to help the process of psychic change. Whatever external factors might be disturbing to us, we are free to apply the light of awareness to our reactions. Once we are conscious of our responses, we can then investigate the inner voices and attitudes that shape this reaction. This investigation provides the psychological space we need to choose our responses, just as we can choose not to scratch an itch once we are aware of the itch and the impulse to scratch. In this way, we become more responsible for ourselves, another mark of maturity.

Being responsible for our reactions does not mean that we are to blame for everything that happens to us. Such thinking is more grandiosity. We will do well in this area to limit ourselves to the following two propositions:

1. Our reactions to events are mediated by our attitudes and beliefs.
2. Our responses to events, regardless of the forces that generated them, are subject to our influence.

As human beings, we have the unique ability to draw meaning from our life experiences. We have the mental capacity to reflect on events and fit them into a world view, or to alter our world view in light of new experiences. When I am disturbed, such as by someone else's behavior, I know that I am up against some limit, some constriction within me that bears investigation. For example, when I see a parent scolding his or her child in a cruel, belittling way, what rises in me at once is anger toward the parent and concern for the child. This is a natural human response—to protect the helpless from harm and to attack the perpetrator of that harm. Common human concern for the welfare of another brings it forth. By learning not to automatically act on that concern, we are not learning to be indifferent to the suffering of others. Rather, we are learning to cultivate our ability to respond with compassion and understanding according to the specific nature of the situation, particularly in highly charged ones. We practice attending to the thoughts and feelings that arise within us, not for the purpose of becoming unmovable, but rather so that our response is chosen rather than automatic. This is the essence of responsibility.

To develop responsibility, however, we must avoid the danger of criticizing ourselves when we find ourselves responding in unskillful but naturally human ways. Certainly, we cannot expect ourselves to hold our heart open with compassion for someone who has caused great harm to our close friend or relative. When we receive news that a person has hurt someone we love, our mind naturally responds with a number of emotions, one of which is invariably anger. It is almost impossible to prevent the arising of anger and, even if we could, it would not necessarily be psychologically healthy to have such control over our emotions. But we can work *with* the feelings, investigating their nature, including the deeper thoughts and motivations producing them.

In addition, when we find rage and vengeance in our heart, at that moment often the best we can do is to engender self-acceptance and compassion for the suffering we experience. This experience arises both from grief occasioned by our loss, and from the pain and fear that come with the rage and vengeance that close our heart.

In most normal situations we have some choice regarding our responses. But choices are ours to make only so long as we know that choice is possible. For much of my life I had no idea that I could choose my responses. I had always thought that emotions arose spontaneously and that the capacity to express them indicated psychological health. This idea was reinforced by much of what I had learned from the human potential movement in psychology. While working the Seventh Step I began to see things differently. I realized that emotional maturity involved more than the ability to recognize and accept whatever thoughts, emotions, and fantasies appeared in my consciousness. It also required developing my capacity for choosing actions that are respectful to myself and others, often irrespective of those inner forces.

This is what it means to practice skillful action, making room for *all* of what I call *self*, which includes integrating the disowned shadow-self, while at the same time treating others with courtesy and respect. This requires allowing all thoughts and emotions into the light of awareness, while consciously choosing which to express. No feeling or thought is judged as bad or wrong, nor are we bad or wrong for having them.

A guide that I have found particularly helpful in this work is Buddhism's Four Noble Truths.[7] After stating that the cause of human suffering is rooted in our inability to perceive that all things are constantly changing, the Buddha explained that the way beyond suffering is to change one's perception. The way to alter one's perception is by following the Buddha's Eightfold Path. Journeying the Eightfold Path involves practicing certain principles that are quite similar to those contained in the Twelve Steps of Alcoholics Anonymous. Let's take a look at two of them: right speech and right action.

Right speech involves not lying, and refraining from using words, such as in gossiping, that would injure or disrupt the peace of others. What an incredibly difficult practice. How can we know what to say when often what we've come to think of as honestly expressing our thoughts and feelings results in hurting someone else? It is a very powerful practice to go through each day so mindful of our speech that we are aware of each impulse to exaggerate or understate.

I have always had a habit of embellishing my stories whenever I described my experiences to others. I told myself I did this to make my experiences more interesting and entertaining to my audience. But often I would change things for no apparent reason. Other times, I would change facts to win an argument with a friend or family member. Unable to justify my dishonesty, I would sometimes forget that I was lying and become indignant when the other person suggested that I was not telling the truth. On other occasions, I would minimize the fact that I was lying by telling myself that these "white lies" did no serious harm.

As part of my work on Step Seven, I began attending closely to what I said to people. Whenever I found myself exaggerating or modifying facts I would force myself to stop speaking. Then I would, often with great difficulty, explain to my listener that I was not being truthful in what I had been saying. I have even had to do this when working with clients who have come to me in therapy. For instance, at times I would share some personal experience in response to an issue a client was working through. As I spoke, I might catch myself trying to appear wiser or in some way better than the actual facts might suggest. Suddenly, I would realize I was lying and a sense of shame would come over me. Recalling my commitment to right speech, to speaking only truthfully, I would stop and acknowledge to my client that I had been exaggerating and did not wish to leave a false impression. I would then restate myself truthfully.

Occasionally, I still have to do this and it continues to be difficult. A part of me screams that it is unprofessional to share such things with clients, reminding me that I shouldn't use the client's hour to work on my character defects. Sometimes, this voice says my client will think I am crazy and will want to leave me for another therapist. It argues that it isn't really a big deal and that I should just forget it.

Sometimes my ego-mind prevails with these arguments. When it does, and I fail to straighten things out, some piece of healing work for both the client and myself is passed over for that time. The wall of isolation is maintained. The client lives with the false security derived from believing his or her therapist is without flaws, a belief that must go sooner or later during the life of our relationship. On my side, the price I pay for reinforcing this illusion is that I continue to live in the painful state of having to maintain a false image of myself. I continue to live in the suffering produced by my inflation, hiding my true self for fear I will be found wanting.

More and more of the time, however, I take the risk and speak the truth. Pushing through the awkwardness occasioned by my honesty, the client and I then have the opportunity to work together to integrate my humanness into our relationship—into our reality. The therapeutic relationship then transcends the safe and familiar and becomes a profound human encounter in which both people are changed.

In addition to the practice of right speech, the Buddha suggests practicing *right action*, which involves, among other things, refraining from intentionally inflicting pain on other living beings. According to some practitioners, such actions may range from killing a bothersome fly to verbally or physically attacking another person. The practice is as much about acting consciously as it is about refraining from hurting living things, the goal being to learn to make deliberate and conscious choices leading to fewer and fewer harmful acts. There may be times when we choose to harm someone—for instance, when protecting oneself or a loved one from attack.

Our commitment is to remain mindful of the effects of our action.

An aspect of *right action* of particular significance for me is the suggestion that one refrain from stealing. Like many other compulsive people I've known, I had taken things that did not belong to me. It makes sense to me that being compulsive would make me prone to thievery when I take into account how driven I've been by the belief that I must always have whatever I want whenever I want it. Is it that we feel entitled not only to take for ourselves more than we actually need but to take things that don't belong to us? My Fourth Step inventory contained many examples of thievery. I made note of people to whom I would eventually have to make financial amends when I got to Steps Eight and Nine. But here in Step Seven, there were important things I could do to further my recovery in preparation for making amends. Most importantly, I could begin by refraining from taking *anything* that did not belong to me.

As I began paying more attention to my intentions and actions in this area, I discovered how often I violated this precept. For instance, I was forced to acknowledge the games I played with magazine publishers. For years I had been in the habit of ordering magazine subscriptions, only half conscious of the fact that I had no intention of maintaining the subscription or paying for it. I would send in the card having checked the box indicating that the publisher should bill me later. Soon I would receive the bill, followed shortly by my first copy of the magazine. After reading the magazine I would throw the bill away. Naturally, the publishing house would stop sending the magazine but continue billing me for the subscription. When the bills continued to come in the mail, I would become incensed, often complaining to my wife that the company had a lot of nerve to keep pestering me. She would innocently point out that I might have been better off had I not ordered the magazine in the first place. Her comments would, of course, infuriate me, adding fuel to my feelings that the whole world was conspiring to make my life miserable.

The Eightfold Path, including right speech and right action, is an effective framework for actively working with character defects. But for me, the central theme of this Step, of working a Twelve Step program as a whole, still comes down to this: while one can by steadfast work effectively change one's character, lasting and genuine spiritual transformation is brought about, not just through one's efforts but through the grace of God. The path of spiritual and psychological growth is a blend of effort and surrender.

Before concluding our discussion of the Seventh Step, let us return to the subject of surrender for a moment. All too easily, we lose sight of the importance of cultivating this attitude when we're caught up in the seemingly more practical business of defining the affirmative steps we can take to modify our character defects. We need to bear in mind, as we approach our shadow sides, that surrender—the yielding aspect of this work—makes its own demands on us. To be capable of surrendering ourselves to our Higher Power as described in the Seventh Step prayer requires self-acceptance and compassion for the person we are at present.

Few of us bring such qualities with us when we first come into a recovery program. Only after a great deal of healing work can we understand that, by humbly asking God to remove our defects of character, we become willing to accept ourselves as we are. We become willing to allow the loving energy of our Higher Power to reduce our self-loathing and elevate our self-esteem. Working through Step Seven, we learn to forgive ourselves. Only after we have begun that important healing work can we effectively move on to the task of making amends to others for harms we have done.

After awareness has brought us to the path of healing, it is forgiveness that softens the path and allows continued progress. . . . Forgiveness allows us to let go of the curtains of resentment, the filters of the mind.

— Stephen Levine

Forgiving others has always been advocated in Christianity, but all too often the need for it is associated with judgment and guilt. In psychotherapy, forgiving oneself is more likely to be emphasized, as in learning to accept and express negative emotions such as anger. Healing the psyche, like healing relationships, however, depends on forgiving both oneself and others.

— Frances Vaughan

Guilt is a self-made poison, which we administer to ourselves frequently. It is the most effective tool the ego has for insuring that we will remain hopelessly bound to our past and therefore not recognize each opportunity the present offers us for our release. There is only one known antidote for guilt: complete forgiveness, starting with ourselves and extending to everyone who shares the world with us.

— Gerald Jampolsky

CHAPTER EIGHT

Making a List of Amends And Becoming Willing To Make Them

Made a list of all persons we had harmed, and became willing to make amends to them all.*

Of all the Steps, the two that disturbed me the most when I first noticed what actions they required were Steps Three and Eight. I have already described my resistance to the word *God* when I came across it in Step Three, and how I was initially put off by references to God at the meetings and their evangelical flavor. Only because I was utterly desperate about my weight and compulsive overeating was I willing to return to the meetings and try to get past my discouragement at the thought of turning my will and life over to God.

The first time I read Step Eight I laughed out loud and thought, *These OA people have to be kidding. Why in hell would I want to make such a list, and why would I ever want to make amends to the people whose names might appear on it?* I had come

---

* Step Eight, the Twelve Steps of Overeaters Anonymous, adapted from the Twelve Steps of Alcoholics Anonymous. The complete Twelve Steps of AA appear on page 221.

to OA to get a new diet and find group support to help me stick to it so I could get and stay thin. How could trying to atone for bad things I had done to others over a period of twenty or thirty years help me lose weight and keep it off?

As I thought about what the Step required, I remembered old friends and former lovers I had mistreated, which brought vague memories of dishonesty, sexual exploitation, theft, and other actions I was not proud of. These memories seemed like vultures waiting to pick at the bones of my already weary and broken ego. *Why bother with this old stuff?* I wondered. *What purpose could there be in dredging up my less-than-noble behaviors toward others, let alone having to contact those people? Couldn't I just let it be water under the bridge and start fresh?*

A common characteristic of people with compulsive behaviors is our tendency to get ahead of ourselves. We want all things to happen on *our* timetable and are terribly impatient with ourselves, with little or no regard for our internal rhythms. Our minds seem to refuse to take things one at a time. That is why so much of the common-sense guidance given in recovery programs comes in the form of terse slogans: First Things First, One Day at a Time, Easy Does It.

Here I was just starting in OA and already I was worrying about the Eighth Step. I hadn't begun to work Step One, and I was already terrified over the prospect of listing all the people I had harmed in the past. Luckily, I had the good sense to talk to a number of old-timers about my concerns over this Step and was comforted to hear that the Steps were written in a particular order for a reason. I was told that we should not undertake the challenge of listing and making amends in the early stages of the Twelve Step process because we have not yet been psychically prepared by the important Steps that precede this task. On the contrary, before engaging in amends work, we must experience the inner changes brought about by systematically working through each preceding

Step. This way, we become capable of making our amends in the right spirit.

When we attempt to make amends before we are grounded in our spiritual program, ulterior motives, such as the desire to ease our conscience and bolster our ego, will result in unskillful, ineffective behavior. Our amends work will then only serve to enhance our feelings of pride and self-righteousness rather than further our spiritual development. To avoid this pitfall, we must have learned the humility that comes with working Steps Six and Seven.

Some people want to start making amends right away, I presume in the hope of quickly clearing their consciences. But most of us, already filled with shame and self-loathing and afraid of exposure and vulnerability, consider the prospect with dread. At the beginning of our recovery work, we have not cultivated sufficient humility and self-forgiveness to allow us to make amends without increasing our shame and sense of unworthiness.

The Twelve Step process moves back and forth between contemplation and action. Beginning with an investigation of the nature of addiction and an admission of powerlessness, we proceed to the inner work of coming to believe a Power greater than ourselves could restore us to sanity. We then commit ourselves to work to bring about a radical change in the source of motivation in our lives from egocentric to spirit centered. With these first three Steps, we develop within ourselves attitudes of honesty, open-mindedness, and willingness so that we can proceed through the action Steps of Four and Five. In these Steps, we write a fearless and searching moral inventory, then share it with someone we believe to be understanding and mature enough to keep our confidence. Once again, in Steps Six and Seven we move inward to engage in contemplative investigation: we explore and cultivate our willingness to commit ourselves to surrender our lifelong reliance on outmoded psychological defenses—those character defects that have been the motivation for actions harmful to ourselves and our relationships with others.

Only after having moved through all these stages are we ready to take the actions called for in Steps Eight and Nine with the appropriate attitude. We can now make our list of people we have harmed from a place of humility and forgiveness. We are prepared to attempt to rectify the damage we have done to others and to our relationships. Done in this spirit, our amends work can move us into deeper contact with our Higher Self.

As I see it, there are three stages to amends work. The *first stage* involves identifying the harms we have done to others. The Twelve and Twelve defines *harm* as "the result of instincts in collision, which cause physical, mental, emotional, or spiritual damage to people."[1] This is what we are searching for in our Step work. We have shifted our attention from how the world has mistreated us to investigating the darker sides of our own psyches—our Shadow. Having put these things in our inventory, we then share them with another person and seek the aid of our Higher Power in bringing about their transformation.

In Steps Eight and Nine we enter the second stage of amends work. Now, we must do something to heal the wounds we have caused others as a result of our egocentric behaviors. To do so, we scan the chronicle of our relationships in our inventory, noting when we acted out of self-centeredness and gave free rein to our negative personality traits. In Step Eight, we list the names of people with whom we were irritable, unreliable, dishonest, and outright abusive.

Then, in Step Nine, we carry out the *second stage* of amends work by taking whatever actions are appropriate and necessary to repair the damage we have done.

The *third stage* of amends work, which continues for the rest of our life, involves our daily attempt to relate in unharmful ways to others in all our affairs. I don't mean by this that we never do or say anything that might upset another person; nor do I mean that we should avoid controversy and struggle. I mean we make a commitment to pay attention to our motivations to ensure that when an encounter is going badly, our actions are not merely *reactions* but responsible conscious choices made for our recovery. The Twelve and Twelve puts it this way: "We consider how, with our newfound knowledge of ourselves, we may develop the best possible relations with every human being we know. . . ."[2]

When I set out to make my list of amends, I made a significant discovery: every time I remembered a person or situation that called for an amend on my part, my mind found objection. First, I would recall a person I had clearly harmed, and I would experience a moment of shame or guilt. Then, I would immediately hear the voice in my head say that I did not need to make amends because *in this particular case my actions were justified.* The argument that I had been mistreated first and was only evening the score came up with almost every person and action I considered putting on my amends list. It was obvious to me that I had rarely done harmful things without substantial provocation; some act or omission on the other person's part always seemed to justify my behavior.

An example comes from a week-long workshop for people interested in using journal writing as a tool for introspection and personal growth I attended long before coming to OA. In addition to the general workshop, a weekend program was offered for mental health professionals who wanted training in the use of journaling in their work with clients. I enrolled in the week-long program, deciding to wait and see how I liked it before committing the additional time and money to the weekend program.

As the week progressed, I found the sessions rather boring. While I did pick up some useful information about keeping a psychological journal, for the most part the experience was very unsatisfying. By the time the general workshop came to an end and the weekend for professionals was approaching, I had strong reservations about attending. Before the main workshop ended, however, the leader made a strong pitch for the weekend program. He explained that he hoped to share valuable information with those who were considering teaching journal writing to clients. Despite my doubts about the leader and his program, my greed—my desire for "special information"—led me to enroll in the weekend workshop.

Almost as soon as the weekend session began, I realized that I had made a poor choice. Those of us who remained for this additional workshop did little more than spend hours writing long essays for the leader, explaining how we envisioned using his journal process in our professional work. I wrote my essays and turned them in along with everyone else, but felt I was being exploited because the leader offered no actual training in the use of this process with clients. The program seemed to be nothing more than a vehicle through which the leader and his organization could draw on the group's collective thoughts about how his process could be used in psychotherapy.

The final insult came during the last session, during which the leader explained that upon his return home he intended to read what we each had submitted. He added, without a hint of embarrassment, that he was developing a professional training program, and if we were interested in enrolling we would have to apply formally and turn over a substantial sum of money. He wanted us to know that the weekend program we were attending was not really part of his training program but was only a means of introducing us to his future plans.

I was furious. My worst suspicions were confirmed—I had been tricked and exploited. The desire for revenge swelled within me. *How can I get even with that S.O.B.?* I thought. *How can I pay him back for trying to screw me?* I tried to think of a way and it came. Throughout the workshop, a table had been set up on which books and audiotapes were offered for sale. I had passed by it often, sometimes stopping to browse the books and examine the topics covered on the audiotapes. Nothing attracted me enough to make a purchase, and I already owned a copy of the basic text written by the leader. But now in my revenge I had to have some of those books and tapes. Suddenly, it seemed fair and reasonable to help myself to a sizable selection from the display. I even decided I needed an extra copy of the leader's book to use as a loaner copy for clients.

During a meal break, when everyone was in the dining room, I slipped into the meeting hall and approached the table. My heart was pounding with fear and excitement as I opened my carrying bag. A small voice within whispering that I shouldn't do this was silenced by a much louder voice exclaiming that I had a right to take avenging action. I began stuffing books and tapes indiscriminately into my bag. Quickly, I closed it and rushed from the hall. My chest was still pounding, but I had such a great sense of satisfaction; stealing the books and tapes had eased my outrage. I could now leave the retreat satisfied that I had gotten even; I had not allowed myself to be exploited.

When I recalled the theft and considered writing down the name of the organization that had put on the journal workshop, my mind immediately protested. *Why the hell are you putting those guys on your amends list? You didn't do anything wrong. You just evened the score after they ripped you off. They are the ones who should be making amends.* Clearly, I had taken something that didn't belong to me and needed to clear my accounts. I started to write. But once again my ego-mind demanded the attention of the court in my head. *Don't be stupid. This Step doesn't mean that you have to pay money to someone who cheated you in the first place. What harm did you do in just balancing the accounts? Forget this one and think of someone you harmed without any justification.* During this first attempt to list my amends, I left this name off the list, persuaded by my feelings of shame and embarrassment that I might make an amend I really didn't have to make.

But as I continued to reflect on whom to put on my list, I continued having the same problem with each person I considered. I turned to the Twelve and Twelve hoping to find guidance and comfort. More accurately, I think I hoped to find justification for not having to make amends to people whom I felt had mistreated me first. The chapter on Step Eight turned out to be disappointing in this regard. Rather than finding support for leaving these people off of my amends list, I discovered that the chapter was devoted in large measure to addressing this kind of thinking. Once again Bill W.'s honest self-examination had led him to insights into the addict's mind that were relevant to my concerns. He and the other early AA's must have experienced intense internal struggles over their amends, seeking ways to avoid making them. In particular, self-justification seemed to serve quite often as a reason to avoid making a particular amend. From his experience Bill wrote:

> *The moment we ponder a twisted or broken relationship with another person, our emotions go on the defensive. To escape looking at the wrongs we have done another, we resentfully focus on the wrong he has done us.*[3]

I was reminded that the addict's mind creates a view of reality that reinforces egocentric thinking. Self-justification, a form of denial regarding the truth about myself and my motivations, kept me from being willing to acknowledge the harms I had done to others. As I struggled with myself over whether to put certain names on my list, I noticed that how I justified keeping them off was similar to how I justified my compulsive overeating. I saw the parallel between the ways my mind would justify taking that first bite and how it justified my unskillful actions with other people. My addict's mind was at work sabotaging my ability to follow through on resolutions and commitments, thwarting any movement toward recovery and psychological maturity.

During my pre-OA days, most often after a weekend of bingeing, I would decide to start a new diet. Filled with shame and remorse over the amount of food I had consumed in the past few days and over the current bloated state of my body, I would resolve to follow a low-calorie diet until I had things "back under control." Starting on Monday morning full of enthusiasm, I would eat a small breakfast, perhaps a piece of whole-wheat toast with cottage cheese and fruit. After the meal, I would feel no hunger, pleased with myself for having established a new eating regime. I was off to a great start. By late morning, I would be pretty hungry; my stomach would occasionally growl, and, periodically, I would feel powerful waves of tension and anxiety. While my clients related their difficulties, my mind would be on other matters—what to do about lunch. Due to the internal dialogue raging in my head, the closer I got to my meal break, the less I could attend to the words and feelings my clients expressed.

My thoughts ran something like this.

Me: *God, am I feeling hungry!*
Addict: *Of course you are. You really didn't eat enough for breakfast. That piece of bread you toasted was actually much smaller than the others in the loaf. That's really one of the problems with buying bread from the health food stores. Those small bakeries don't make loaves with uniform slices. If you had allowed yourself two pieces you wouldn't be hungry now.*
Me: *But I am trying to diet. . . . What did Nancy just say about the fight she and her husband had last night? I'm having a hard time paying attention. I wonder if she can tell. . . . Damn it, I'm angry about feeling hungry. Or am I ashamed over the fact that Nancy is paying me to listen and help her and all I can think of is what I am going to have for lunch.*
Addict: *Don't get so upset. Of course you are having a hard time. Anyone would if they had eaten such a small breakfast. Everything will be all right when you have eaten lunch. . . . When you have finished with Nancy, let's go out for a nice meal.*

Me: (with no conviction whatsoever) *But I brought my diet lunch.*

Addict: *Just leave it in the refrigerator. Don't you feel better thinking about getting out of the office and eating at Joe's Burgers? Just don't eat anything fattening. . . . Maybe a salad with oil and vinegar dressing on the side. . . . Just don't order a cheeseburger with fries.*

Me: *I guess that would be okay. The thought of going out for lunch is making me feel better.*

As this discussion winds down, I return the focus of my attention to Nancy's words. I am feeling much calmer now, knowing that shortly I will be eating lunch. I picture myself at a table in Joe's Burgers. I even see the plate of food in front of me, but I cannot make out what is on the plate. A salad? A hamburger with fries? I experience a moment of doubt and fear, but it passes as soon as I think about how pleasant it will be to eat at Joe's. The dialogue continues.

Me: *Maybe I should just stay in the office and eat the lunch I made this morning. After all, I'm on a diet.*

Addict: *Will you stop worrying? Everything will be fine. Trust me. You'll be glad you decided to go out for lunch. Remember, you're going to have a low-calorie salad. Nothing wrong with that, is there?*

Sitting in Joe's examining the menu, I glance around the restaurant at other people eating. I can't help noticing what is on their plates. Hamburgers with french fries. Lasagne with garlic bread. Suddenly, I am aware of the sweet, overpowering smells of garlic and onions sautéing in the kitchen. Another short dialogue runs through my head.

Me: *I know I should have Joe's Greek Salad, but it doesn't seem like enough. Besides, I think it is unfair that all those people can eat whatever they want while I have to eat a crummy little salad.*

Addict: (speaking like my oldest and dearest friend)

You're right. It isn't fair. Besides, a salad won't be enough to hold you until dinner. All you will get will be maybe two ounces of cheese and an olive or two. The rest will be just some damned lettuce, and if you spend that much you want more than a plate of lettuce. Go ahead and eat something substantial so you won't be hungry this afternoon. Then just go light with dinner tonight.

When the waitress arrives to take my order, I pause momentarily. The moment of truth has arrived. The truth is that what I will do has never been in doubt. Even as I was promising myself on Sunday night that I was going to start a diet and stick to it, this moment of failure was a certainty. Looking at the menu I see the words, "Joe's Greek Salad," and at the same moment I hear myself saying, "Cheeseburger with a side of fries, please."

Before recovery, when it came to food and eating, I invariably gave in to the addict. I did so without ever comprehending that its voice was a rather constant feature of my inner world. During my years in OA, I have become familiar with this voice and often refer to it as *The Tempter*. I have also come to see that it speaks to me in many areas besides food and eating. Whatever the issue, *The Tempter* always seems able to offer good reasons for doing things a reasonable person might not think such a good idea. For instance, whenever I experience the impulse to buy something and I attempt to deny myself, *The Tempter* joins the discussion going on in my head. It always seems to be my friend and ally, seeking only my happiness. No matter what my current financial situation is, or the fact that I have little or no need for the particular item I covet, *The Tempter* coaxes me to treat myself, speaking with words I long to hear: "Go ahead; you'll feel better." And, in the short run, I do feel better, calmer, satiated.

Once I have given in to my desire and leave the store with my prize, the addict, who only moments before was my comforting friend, suddenly becomes my mortal enemy. Having succumbed to my impulses and satisfied my desire, I begin to hear the stinging accusations of what I had taken to be my caring and loyal comrade. My buying frenzy completed, my ally, *The Tempter*, suddenly changes into *The Judge*. Now, with a mercilessly condemning voice, it attacks me for being weak willed and stupid. *How could you?* it asks with bitter contempt. *I thought you were trying to save money. You really blew it this time. You needed that TV like you needed a hole in your head. What a jerk you are.* I am filled with shame and self-loathing, defenseless against its stinging blows.

This is the addictive cycle well described by Dr. Silkworth in his introductory comments at the beginning of the Big Book. In "The Doctor's Opinion" he explains it this way:

> *Men and women drink essentially because they like the effect produced by alcohol. The sensation is so elusive that, while they admit it is injurious, they cannot after a time differentiate the true from the false. . . . They are restless, irritable and discontented, unless they can again experience the sense of ease and comfort which comes at once by taking a few drinks—drinks which they see others taking with impunity. After they have succumbed to the desire again, as so many do, and the phenomenon of craving develops, they pass through the well-known stages of a spree, emerging remorseful, with a firm resolution not to drink again.*[4]

This was not only my experience with eating, but also with buying and other compulsive behaviors that I was powerless to control.

And I was just as powerless over the forces within that argued that I did not have to make an amend to the people who ran the journal workshop whose books and tapes I had stolen. My resistance to putting them on my amends list was overwhelming. I did not want to contact the journal workshop people, nor did I wish to send them money for the tapes and books. My addict spoke loud and clear: *Not only were you morally justified in taking them, but you didn't even get much out of reading the books and listening to the tapes!* I seemed unable to go forward. Once again, I turned to others in the program and to AA literature for help.

Eventually, my resistance softened as I came to realize that making amends to people I had harmed was primarily for my benefit and only incidentally for the other person's. I learned that the purpose of making amends was not to make others happy; it was to complete my unfinished business with people I had harmed in the past. Amends were necessary to relieve me of the psychic burden of guilt over what I had done and the fear that others might do the same to me. I understood that, while making amends involved interpersonal relationships on one level—as does all Twelve Step work—it also involved inner work to clear the channel between my conscious self and my Higher Power.

In the end, as I made my amends list I included the organization that had run the journal workshop. My recovery was too important to me by this time to omit them. I was accustomed to the many forms of resistance and justification that my mind used to dissuade me from carrying out the suggestions of the Twelve Steps, and I would not be impeded by these forces of regression. I intended to continue moving along the spiritual path that began with my admission of powerlessness over my compulsive desires to overeat. I had come too far and had received too many benefits from this new way of life to do otherwise.

None of the major schools of psychotherapy explicitly suggest the patient go to people they have harmed and make amends. Quite the contrary, most therapists work from the premise that what is most important in therapy is to identify ways the patient was mistreated by significant people, especially in childhood. Certainly, a part of any successful therapy experience is to identify and integrate repressed feelings from parental and societal mistreatment, whether that mistreatment was intentional or not. Harm done to us by our principal caretakers during our formative years of infancy and early childhood is the soil in which our character defects take root. Most of us saw that fact starkly when we wrote our Fourth Step inventory. We remembered painful incidents in the face of which we developed many of our character defects. Then, they seemed to serve as protection from an apparently hostile world. But these defenses were to evolve into habitual attitudes and behaviors that masked and misdirected our powerful emotions, still suppressed in the shadows of our psyche.

One of the therapist's roles in the therapeutic process is to help the client address the cognitive, emotional, or behavioral effects of the harm suffered in his or her family of origin. Also, the therapist helps to identify the feelings that were subsequently repressed. To the extent we are unable to experience and express our sadness, anger, hurt, and fear, we are limited in our capacity to experience and express our joy and pleasure. This is due to the walls we have erected between our consciousness and our bodily sensations and emotions. We are only partially alive. A therapeutic experience allows us to recall those significant negative childhood experiences and work through the repressed emotions attached to them. In this way, we become free to respond to current life issues with new flexibility and spontaneity.

This is why any attempt at "spiritual-growth work" on the pretence of ridding oneself of ego is courting disaster. We need, instead, to establish a healthy ego. It is only a healthy, flexible ego, an ego forged by the humility of acknowledging and integrating the disowned aspects of our character (the Shadow), that does not require inflation and protection against the world. Once a healthy ego is established, we can place it in the service of our Higher Self and travel the path toward Wholeness.

We must move beyond the blaming that keeps us in the illusion that the past is the problem. This illusion is the problem in that so long as we live under its yoke, we are cut off from the freedom that forgiveness will bring us.

Forgiveness cannot be forced; healing has its own rhythm and timing. After earlier Steps involving self-forgiveness, Step Eight brings us to one of the most important challenges of spiritual healing—cultivating forgiveness of others. This was the central lesson for me in making my list of amends. I couldn't put a name down until I could find sufficient forgiveness in my heart. I came to understand that forgiveness did not mean I now condoned harmful and sometimes even cruel acts done to me. Rather it meant that I no longer wished to allow resentment and guilt to keep my heart frozen and closed.

Forgiveness means resolution, completion. To make amends is to forgive: to forgive is to complete the work of the past so that we can experience the present with a freshness of vision and an openness of heart. Bill W. put it this way:

> *In many instances we shall find that though the harm done others has not been great, the emotional harm we have done ourselves has. Very deep, sometimes quite forgotten, damaging emotional conflicts persist below the level of consciousness. At the time of these occurrences, they may actually have given our emotions violent twists which have since discolored our personalities and altered our lives for the worse.[5]*

Much of the discussion on the Eighth Step in the Twelve and Twelve focuses on the need for a close examination of our personality traits. While restitution is paramount, "it is equally necessary that we extricate from an examination of our personal relations every bit of information about ourselves and our fundamental difficulties that we can."[6] We are encouraged to recognize how our personality traits set off unpleasant reactions in others. This does not mean we must bear responsibility for how others behave, but it does direct us to examine how our attitudes and behaviors contribute to a breakdown in our interpersonal relationships. We are called upon to take responsibility for our part in bringing about a deterioration in our relationship to another person, without regard to the other's contribution.

As I reflected on the effect my mistrust and dishonesty had on others, I recognized that I had learned to control and manipulate people through either temper tantrums or passive sulking. It was obvious that so long as I continued to behave in relationships as though other people merely existed to fulfill my needs, I could expect others to disappoint and frustrate me. In making my amends list, I had to do more than look for the obvious harm I had done to others; I had to identify the *patterns of interaction* by which I damaged my relationships and left those who were on the receiving end feeling hurt, angry, and confused. I realized that at the same time I was listing those I had harmed, I was also letting go of some of the defensiveness and tension that had been part of my way of relating to the world.

Preparing to face those I had harmed meant surrendering much of the guilt, suspicion, and resentments I had accumulated throughout my life. Here again, I saw that I was engaged in the kind of forgiveness work described by Arthur Egendorf in his book about healing from the psychological wounds suffered in the Vietnam War: "I would forgive—not in response to a promise that it wouldn't happen again, but as a gift, as an ennobling act, the only act that had the power to be thoroughly healing for me."[7]

Looking over my amends list, I knew that my character defects, not the behavior of others, had motivated my actions. I had come to recognize the extent to which my relationships with others had been affected by my pride, greed, envy, jealousy, resentments, lust, and self-pity. By working Steps Five, Six, and Seven, I had cultivated some compassion for myself and others, some deep understanding of how hard it is to live in a less-than-perfect world with limited physical, mental, and emotional resources. As my defenses softened, my capacity for compassion grew, and I could accept myself as just one person doing the best he could in a world of others doing the same. More and more I could see other people, not as evil, dangerous forces but as wounded children like myself, trying to find peace and security in an oftentimes difficult and painful world.

This shift in consciousness did not mean that I had to allow others to abuse me. It was still important for me to set psychological and physical boundaries. However, I was learning that at the same time I asserted my needs and protected myself from the unskillful actions of others, I could remind myself that behind the unpleasant and unskillful surface activity was a spark of the Divine and another wounded person.

There is a wonderful Chinese story that has helped me with this work. It tells of a boatman rowing up a river in the fog. Suddenly, he sees through the swirling mist another boat moving downstream toward his. Frantically, he tries to alter his course, shouting at the other boatman to avoid the impending collision. As the other boat continues moving toward him, he grows angrier and angrier at the apparent indifference of the other boatman, calling him a fool and an idiot. His fury reaches its peak as the boats collide. Then, as the boats drift together momentarily, he sees that the other boat is empty; it had come loose from its moorings and drifted downstream. When he discovers there's no one to blame, the man's anger dissipates.

We can forgive more readily to the extent we are able to surrender our belief that other people are intending us harm. How much easier and gentler my relationships are when I work from the assumption that the other person is doing the best he or she can at the moment. This new attitude means that, even when I ask other people to change their behaviors, I am capable of maintaining a sense of caring and compassion for the person behind the behavior. And from this new posture, I am finally ready to approach the task of making amends for the harm I have done others as a result of acting from my character defects; I am ready to face Step Nine.

If the doors of perception were cleansed, everything would appear to man as it is, infinite. For man has closed himself up, till he sees all through the narrow chinks of his cavern.

— William Blake

Pain, suffering, and grief will continue to be felt—but they will be attenuated, not magnified, by a new view of the world. We shall learn to participate in grief and pain from an utterly new perspective. It will be a perspective that modifies the meaning we impart to the experience, without eliminating the experience itself. For we know that the emotional and cognitive components to experience are decidedly transmutable to other qualities, qualities which can transform sorrow, pain, and grief. In such a process the fact of the experience remains; the event is not destroyed—it is the meaning that is imparted to it that is everything.

— Larry Dossey, M.D.

When people who were never particularly strong become strong in the face of adversity, when people who tended to think only of themselves become unselfish and heroic in an emergency, I have to ask myself where they got these qualities which they would freely admit they did not have before. My answer is that this is one of the ways in which God helps us when we suffer beyond the limits of our own strength.

— Harold Kushner

CHAPTER NINE

Making Amends

*Made direct amends to such people wherever possible, except when to do so would injure them or others.**

When I finished my amends list, it was time to "go out to our fellows and repair the damage done in the past."[1] I interpreted this to mean that I was supposed to be willing to do whatever the circumstances and the person might require. But the truth was, not only was I still not completely willing to make amends to everyone on my list, I was extremely anxious about just contacting most of them. In fact, a few of them were among the very last people on earth I had ever hoped to see again. However, to complete Step Nine, I would not only have to see them again but also have to admit I had caused them harm by my greed, pettiness, and other ignoble motivations. As if that was not enough, I would then have to attempt what was required to make restitution.

My mind balked at the prospect. How shameful to expose myself like that. Surely it was not necessary that I sacrifice all dignity and grovel at people's feet, just because I had caused them some harm long before I understood what I was doing.

* Step Nine, the Twelve Steps of Overeaters Anonymous, adapted from the Twelve Steps of Alcoholics Anonymous. The complete Twelve Steps of AA appear on page 221.

Wasn't I crazy back then? Why not let bygones be bygones? After all, I was becoming a different person as a result of my Step work, and I wouldn't do those things now. My old resentments and fears were greatly diminished, and I was much less sensitive to criticism and disappointment. I was more patient with my family and people with whom I came in contact during the course of my day. *Why dig up the ghosts of the past?* I thought. Despite my ego-mind's efforts to dissuade me, however, I knew that I had to press forward; the only real question worth asking was not *why?* but *how?*

When I asked other people how they had gone about this, I learned there were many approaches, but on some things everyone seemed to agree. For instance, everyone with whom I spoke and everything I read affirmed that restitution must be offered when theft was involved. In years past, particularly during my college years, I had stolen merchandise from various stores. And, of course, there was the business of the books and tapes I had stolen from the workshop. It was suggested that, in order to make a complete amend, I should either go to the store, explain my business, and pay for the items taken, or at least write an explanatory letter enclosing a check to cover what I had stolen.

Making these kinds of amends was not particularly difficult for me. Most of them could be made in relative anonymity, and the amount of money I had to pay was never substantial. In fact, when I looked at the list, I saw that the things I had stolen were never very expensive. They were always small items sitting on a counter or shelf which, for no particular reason, caught my eye and whetted my desire. I would see them and instantly, a voice—my *Tempter*—insisted that I would be justified in taking the object without paying. Then, suddenly, driven by powerful possessive impulses and my compulsion to break the rules and experience that rush of excitement and fear, I would slip the thing into my pocket. Paperback books. Cheap fountain pens. A jar of spices. So much junk, most of which I rarely used. To think, in those acts of petty thievery

I had placed in jeopardy my reputation, my career, and even my freedom. How crazy I was, how out of control. And my denial was so complete, I never realized it.

More difficult were the amends I had to make to intimates and acquaintances with whom I had compromised a relationship. The thought of making these amends brought up my shame and guilt, long repressed from consciousness, which I now had to experience and work through. I had brought these feelings to awareness, having admitted my unskillful thoughts and actions to myself, my Higher Power, and another person. But it was now time to account for what I had done to the people I had actually harmed. Awareness was not enough, according to the experiences of those who contributed to the Big Book. I had to take the action called for in Step Nine if I was ever to live without the crippling feelings of shame, guilt, and fear, and experience anything like a psychic transformation or spiritual awakening.

When I did admit my imperfections and selfish motivations to the people who had been harmed by my unskillful actions, I discovered incredible peace and self-forgiveness. As I worked my way through my amends list, I felt my lifelong feelings of inadequacy and fear of other people's judgments dissolving. I began to find the humility, courage, and honesty necessary to transcend the very character defects that had been the cause of my harmful actions.

Many readers will no doubt view what I am saying with skepticism, a skepticism I shared until I experienced this shift in consciousness. I assure you no one could have been more doubting than I. Nothing in my life experience or world view prepared me for the changes that were taking place within me. But the fact remained that as a result of following the suggestions of these Steps, I was experiencing a radical transformation in myself, significant enough that I was able to do things that had been inconceivable before I began the process of recovery.

For example, before I came to Overeaters Anonymous no one could have convinced me that one day I would go to my ex-wife and *with all sincerity* express my regret for all of the unkindness I had shown her during our marriage and in the stormy years after our divorce. To say that I couldn't stand her would have been putting it mildly. We had fought throughout our marriage, and after our separation and divorce we continued battling with each other, principally over issues related to our son. Much of our animosity was driven by the desperate need on both of our parts to feel in the right, to have the other person admit being in the wrong. Behind every struggle over scheduling our son's visits, for example, was the need each of us had to feel superior to the other. And, at the same time, we unconsciously hoped to hear the other say, "I understand you. I know how hard you are trying, I see that you are doing the best you can. I respect and appreciate you." Neither of us could stretch far enough, take pause long enough to hear the other's unexpressed plea for recognition and comfort, to feel these things for the other, and so, neither of us ever felt comforted.

When making most of my amends, I followed the procedure suggested in the Big Book. First, I contacted the person I had harmed and explained that I was in a recovery program for compulsive overeaters, and that part of my recovery necessitated making amends for harms I had done to people in the past. Having completed that introduction, I named what I saw as my responsibility and asked what action I might perform to set things right.

However, in making amends to my ex-wife I did not attempt to accomplish the task in one encounter. Rather, I began inserting caring and respectful comments in our phone conversations. Occasionally, where it seemed natural, I would tell her I realized that I had been difficult to deal with over the years and that she had tried very hard to balance her needs against mine. The more I said these things, the warmer and gentler she became. And so did I, realizing the more I said them, the more I saw the truth. Sometimes I would note tension or irritation in her voice on the phone. Rather than respond in kind, I reminded myself that she could not harm me and that inside her, just as within myself, there was a frightened child who often showed itself through anger and bitterness. I reminded myself that I did not have to respond to her harshness, but could choose to speak to the wounded child I knew existed within her.

There were moments when I could not keep to my course, and I fell into old patterns of defensiveness and hostility. But over time tensions between us eased. Flare-ups continued to occur when one of us would unintentionally strike a sensitive nerve in the other, but as the months passed, our infrequent phone contacts began to have a gentler quality. My ex-wife seemed less frightened, less hard, and I felt more relaxed. Now and again, we even found ourselves laughing together as our phone conversations became increasingly marked by expressions of appreciation and understanding. We continued treating each other with more courtesy and sincere friendliness. I would never have thought such a thing possible, given the depths of hatred and bitterness that had grown between us. And yet the most tortured relationship of my life became transformed into one of kindness and mutual respect.

For most of my life I had a rule that I never said I was sorry for anything I did. If I intentionally harmed someone, apologizing seemed to be merely a way to avoid responsibility and to prevent the aggrieved person from getting angry at me. On one hand, in my twisted way of thinking, I felt that saying I was sorry somehow implied that I had not *intended the act*. On the other hand, if I had not intended to hurt the person by my actions, I was not responsible, and to say I was sorry made no sense. By means of this convoluted philosophical construction, I managed to turn my fear of exposure, shame, and guilt into a positive concept of mature responsibility.

Early in recovery I learned to see things differently. I came to realize the appropriateness of saying I was sorry when my harmful action was intentional. Where I had knowingly acted in a hurtful manner, making amends seemed to be a sensible course of action. I thereby learned that it was appropriate to apologize when I lost my temper and said unkind things or when I failed to follow through on a commitment.

But Step Nine didn't call for apologizing to people I offended in the present; it directed me to seek out and make amends to people from the past I had harmed. Slowly, I worked through my list of amends. Wherever possible I made my amends in person. When I needed to make amends to someone who was no longer living, I wrote them a letter and made a commitment not to treat others as I had treated them. For those too far away to make face-to-face amends practical, I either called or wrote a letter.

Some of the encounters turned out to be rather tense and unpleasant. In fact, a number of those to whom I offered amends refused to talk to me and some expressed open hostility. These encounters were somewhat painful and embarrassing. But while they were occurring and afterward, I experienced a sense of peace and calm. My recovery work had led me to understand how justified these people were because of how I had treated them. Once the conversations were behind me, I felt a wonderful sense of completion and freedom. I no longer had to live in fear of running into anyone from my past. I had taken what measures I could with everyone that I had reason to believe I had harmed through actions motivated by my character defects. I had done what I could to correct the balance, to right the wrongs.

Most of the people I contacted were surprisingly warm and welcoming. When I explained the nature and purpose of my call or request to meet with them, they expressed willingness to help me clear things up. All but a few said they didn't recall the incidents of which I spoke and only remembered the good times we had spent together. The conversation itself served as the amend as we reflected together on whatever had made our past relationship meaningful to each of us. There was so much healing—a softening of our hearts. To give you a sense of what I mean, let me share with you one of the most powerful of my amend encounters.

I arrived one morning at my office to find several messages on my answering machine. As I went through them, I was surprised to hear the voice of an old friend with whom I had worked many years before. Her message explained that our former mutual employer, whom I'll call Pat, was in a local hospital, gravely ill with cancer. Pat and I had worked together for four very intense and stormy years in the early seventies. She was the executive director and I the clinical director of a multifaceted social service agency providing counseling and educational services to troubled adolescents and their families. A brilliant and energetic person, she was extremely creative and dynamic, with extraordinary native political instinct. At the same time, she was determined to have things her way, often, it seemed to me, ruthless in her efforts to maintain control of everything in which she was involved. When we were on the same side of a struggle, we made a powerful and resourceful team. When we disagreed, a battle would ensue, and, invariably, I would lose.

During the four years we worked together we built an effective and dynamic agency that grew in staff size and range of services year after year. It soon became a model program for delivering effective, cost-efficient social services to troubled youth and families, and Pat and I began to be hailed as innovators in the field of youth services. But behind the public image of a synergistic team, we fought over everything, from budget to staff hiring procedures. We engaged in a destructive battle of wills and a struggle for dominance that affected the entire agency.

Finally, after four years of frustration over repeated defeats, I announced my decision to leave the agency to start a private practice. Pat expressed shock and unhappiness over my decision, but I knew that she was relieved that I was leaving. In hindsight, I understand that she wanted to save everyone the discomfort of facing the truth about how much anger we felt toward each other. She hoped to keep up appearances and make our parting graceful without public expression of our mutual bitterness.

But I would not allow her that last victory, and when the agency staff began planning a farewell party in my honor, I asked that Pat not be invited. I made it clear that I would not participate if she were invited, and despite the protests of a number of staff people, Pat was not invited to the party. I tried to justify myself to the staff, but was successful in convincing only myself that my sole motivation was a desire to avoid duplicity. I had completely repressed the fact that my true motivation was the desire for revenge, to punish her for defeating me so often, for being more clever and powerful than I. The party came and went and soon after, I left the agency. Pat and I barely spoke during those last few weeks and, once I had left, we did not speak to each other again until the day, twelve years later, when I received the message on my machine informing me she was in a hospital.

Pat was one of the first people I had placed on the amends list I made in Step Eight. And yet, as I crossed off the names from that list, one by one, her name remained untouched. It was almost a year after I began making my amends that I received the call informing me that she was in the hospital. As I sat in my office, replaying the message on my phone machine, I felt urgency to contact her. I got the phone number from information and, without thinking about what I was going to say, I dialed the hospital. When the receptionist answered, I asked to be connected to Pat's room. The phone started to ring and continued to ring for a while as I became lost in memories of some of the joyous and painful moments we had shared.

After what must have been quite some time, I was startled out of my reverie by the sound of someone picking up the phone at the other end. I heard the thin and brittle voice of what sounded like a very old woman. *This can't be Pat,* I thought. *She must be in her early fifties now, and this person is probably in her late eighties or even older. I must have reached the wrong room.* I apologized for disturbing her, explaining that I was trying to reach Pat so-and-so's room and asked whether she might be sharing a phone with my friend. The person on the other end explained that she was Pat and asked to whom was she speaking. My voice caught in my throat; nevertheless, I forced a response. I simply said Phillip, certain she would know who I was.

Now it was her turn to express surprise. I assumed that her response of shock related to the fact that she was hearing the voice of someone she hadn't spoken to in years, but I was soon to discover her shock had another source. She asked how I managed to get through to her room, and I explained that the switchboard had simply put me through. She replied, "All of my calls have been carefully screened since I've been in the hospital. No one other than my immediate family has been allowed to ring my room. Not even people on my staff at the agency have spoken to me for the past two weeks. I'm surprised that you were able to get through. Well, to be honest, now that I think about it I'm not so surprised. I guess it's about time for us to talk."

I felt those tingling sensations you get along the spine when you suddenly find yourself in the midst of a strange set of coincidences. If her calls had been so carefully screened, why was I put through? Why didn't I hang up after five or six rings? I must have let the phone ring for several minutes while I was lost in thought. I pulled out of my momentary reflections and explained that I did not want to take much of her time and asked if she was up to a short conversation. She said she was and I continued.

I told her that I had received word of her illness and wanted to express my concern. I struggled to bring myself to the topic of amends, but it took me a while to warm to my task. Finally, I pushed myself toward my goal and explained somewhat sheepishly that the purpose of my call was to make amends to her for my part in our past struggles and for any harm I caused her over the years. Specifically, I wished to make amends for not taking my leave from the agency, from her, with more grace and respect for all that we had done over the period we had worked together.

Before I could say more, she interrupted me and explained that she intended to be out of the hospital in a week or so and suggested that perhaps we could talk more when she got home. I wasn't certain what to say next. From the sound of her voice, I thought that she must have been dying and that she would not be leaving the hospital to go home. And yet, from her comments, I realized that she had not come to terms with the immediacy of her death. I heard the Pat I had once known; her fighting spirit was still both her greatest asset and her biggest liability. In a flash, I was witness to her need to see things the way she wanted them to be, rather than as they were, and her desire to shape the course of events based on her perception of what the situation demanded.

For a moment I felt the urge to make her face the truth about things. I wanted us to be honest with each other. How quickly the familiar patterns reasserted themselves, even after so long a separation; even in the face of death I wanted to make her see things as I did. But I had changed. Despite the impulse to force her to see the truth of her situation, I let it go and said that if she would like to get together when she got out of the hospital, I would be glad to visit her then. I realized that I wouldn't be able to say everything I would have liked; nevertheless, I softly explained that it would mean a great deal to me if she would allow me the opportunity to say a few things while we were still on the phone together. In a playful spirit, I added something about how communication between us had always been a problem, and so we really should take advantage of the fact that despite the obstacles, we were on the phone together. She laughed and invited me to continue.

I began by acknowledging that, over time, I had come to understand that I had been very difficult to work with. I admitted that I had always had a strong desire for power and control but that I had never been able or willing to own these impulses. Pat remained silent as I told her that I had come to realize that my motives, which always seemed pure and honorable to me, were often, in fact, expressions of my desire to feel important and have things run according to my plan. I admitted that I had often tried to get my way at the agency in an attempt to consolidate my power and to enhance my status. I concluded by expressing regret over my behavior toward her—in particular, for having been small-minded and unkind when I had refused her an invitation to my farewell party. I asked if I could say or do anything that might redress the harm my actions had caused.

A sense of warmth and peacefulness came over me; tears were pouring down my cheeks. Pat was also crying softly as she responded. She admitted having been deeply hurt by me and added that it meant a great deal to be able to hear from me after so long a silence. She added that my impulsiveness and aggressiveness had always frightened her and, even though I had often been correct in my assessment of things, she had felt protective of herself and the agency. She concluded by telling me that even though the program had continued to grow and flourish after I left, she had always considered the years we worked together the most exciting and creative in the program's history.

I had an incredible sense of intimacy with her in that moment. We were sharing from the heart in a way we had never been able to in all the years we had worked together. The silences between our words were filled with tenderness and respect, as we acknowledged that, for all our struggles and mistrust of each other, we had loved and cared for each other at one time.

As our conversation wound down, I heard myself say spontaneously, "I'll pray for you." I didn't know how that sounded to her, but I was startled to hear such words coming from my mouth. Pat seemed unruffled as she thanked me for my prayers. There was a silence. She said she would call when she got out of the hospital and suggested that if I wanted to be informed of her progress, I could call the agency for reports. We said good-bye and I hung up the phone. When I called the agency the following day to learn how she was doing, I was told that Pat had died only a few hours after our conversation.

The Big Book suggests that the primary purpose of making amends is not to obtain forgiveness from those we have harmed. We hope that, by making our amends, we improve our relationship with the person to whom we make them. In addition, we hope that the other person comes away from the encounter less fearful and resentful. But the central motivation for making our amends is because *such actions transform us*. As the Big Book puts it, "At the moment we are trying to put our lives in order. But this is not an end in itself. Our real purpose is to fit ourselves to be of maximum service to God and the people about us."[2]

The primary objective of amends work, as with all efforts we make in behalf of recovery, is the broadening of our conscious contact with our Higher Power in order to advance our spiritual awakening. We accomplish this objective by clearing the channel that has been blocked by our character defects. Our direction and guidance come from the still, silent voice within, and we must work to become quiet enough to hear its message.

To be capable of healthier, more satisfying relationships with others, we must be capable of recognizing those character traits that interfere with our natural impulse toward compassion and concern for our fellow human beings. Shame, which in turn generates feelings of unworthiness and inadequacy, begins to dissolve as we shift the source of our motivation from egocentricity to the prompting of our Higher Self. Old resentments begin to dissolve as we identify our part in past unpleasantness, and find the capacity of forgiveness in our heart both toward others and ourselves.

Fear and hatred of others, as we have seen, are often products of our projection of our Shadow onto others. We have come to fear others because we see in them personality traits that we share but have had to deny as our own because of our feelings of guilt and shame. Making amends helps us reduce our fear of others and melts the hatred that had hardened our heart. As we take the actions to heal our relationships, we heal spiritually from within, thus heightening our capacity for living more fully in each unfolding moment.

When I was preparing to make my amends, I asked my sponsor, "What about people who cannot be found or who are no longer living?" He suggested that I make what are called living amends. He explained that a living amend involves taking actions in the present that express our intention to avoid causing to others the kind of harm done to that person. For instance, if we were cold and harsh toward someone who is now no longer living, we might commit ourselves to treat other people with kindness and warmth. Undertaken as a practice in awareness and consciousness rather than a strict rule of behavior, the living amend becomes a powerful vehicle for spiritual growth. Living amends are also useful in changing our current relationships. In addition to expressing regret for things we have done in the past, we can silently commit ourselves to acting in more skillful ways in the future, asking our Higher Self to aid us in this endeavor. The Big Book puts it this way:

> Yes, there is a long period of reconstruction ahead. We must take the lead. A remorseful mumbling that we are sorry won't fill the bill at all. We ought to sit down with the family and frankly analyze the past as we now see it, being very

> *careful not to criticize them. Their defects may be glaring,*
> *but the chances are that our own actions are partly respon-*
> *sible. So we clean house with the family, asking each morn-*
> *ing in meditation that our Creator show us the way of*
> *patience, tolerance, kindliness and love.*[3]

The Big Book's discussion of Step Nine closes with a group of promises referred to as the *Promises of the Program.*[4] They fall into two groups, those which come to fruition as one commences making amends and those that are fulfilled during the working of Step Ten. The two differ significantly. The first set of promises encompasses the psychological and emotional changes brought about by working the Steps – the radical alteration in personality required if one is to live free from the ravages of one's compulsion. The second set of promises refers more specifically to lifting the obsession to drink (or overeat, or act in other compulsive ways). The personality changes are promised first; once they occur, the obsession can be lifted. Here again the Big Book tells us how recovery works: First the personality of the addict is transformed, then the obsession to take the first drink (pill or bite) is lifted. We must first experience the changes in personality promised in Step Nine. Then we will find ourselves able to choose not to engage in those destructive behaviors over which we had no control at the beginning of our journey of recovery.

The message of the Big Book is this: as we begin making our amends, having worked through the previous Steps, we notice changes that have been taking place within us all along. The promised changes are so central to what the program offers that I will quote them in their entirety:

> *If we are painstaking about this phase of our development,*
> *we will be amazed before we are half way through. We are*
> *going to know a new freedom and a new happiness. We will*
> *not regret the past nor wish to shut the door on it. We will*
> *comprehend the word serenity and we will know peace. No*
> *matter how far down the scale we have gone, we will see how*

our experience can benefit others. That feeling of uselessness and self-pity will disappear. We will lose interest in selfish things and gain interest in our fellows. Self-seeking will slip away. Our whole attitude and outlook upon life will change. Fear of people and of economic insecurity will leave us. We will intuitively know how to handle situations which used to baffle us. We will suddenly realize that God is doing for us what we could not do for ourselves.

Are these extravagant promises? We think not. They are being fulfilled among us—sometimes quickly, sometimes slowly. They will always materialize if we work for them.[5]

Notice we are not promised wealth, happiness, or a wonderful lover. We are not told that our life will be free from pain and sorrow, loneliness, or grief. What we are promised is this: through our willingness and efforts to grow spiritually, we will become capable of living a meaningful, useful life, despite our human imperfections and the fact that we exist in a world that is ultimately unpredictable. The world does not change as a consequence of our Twelve Step work. We are not promised divine intervention in the events of our life because of our devotion to God or because we proclaim His power and glory. Rather it is we who change—our attitudes and personalities are transformed so that we face life's challenges in new ways. Again, our new perspective comes not from some external God, but from our commitment to open ourselves to the deeper truths about the nature of reality and the human experience.

Upon working Step Nine we find ourselves living more gently and lightly in the world, less upset by life's inherent difficulties. In fact, that realization enables us to bring more love and compassion both to ourselves and others than might otherwise be possible. We have had vital, transformative spiritual experiences that have allowed us to perceive the world with new eyes. We are not merely playing with new ideas and philosophical ruminations, we are beginning to see things differently. We are being liberated from the narrow view of reality that has shaped and beclouded our experiences; we are glimpsing the true nature of things that we had always been unable to see because the forces of our ego-mind had distorted our perception. We are Waking Up, Coming Home, Entering the Kingdom of Heaven: all metaphors for a transformation that can only be known through direct experience, only hinted at by language and poetic image.

*The ego's unconsciousness heals frequently through reve-
lation and telling of secrets, but the secret connection
with the Self is revealed through enactment of ethical ob-
ligations learned and remembered in secret consort with
the Self.*

— *Russell Lockart*

*The acid that tests gold is there, and the one who judges
    jewels.*
*And the music from the strings no one touches, and the
    source of all water.*
If you want the truth, I will tell you the truth:
Friend, listen: The God whom I love is inside.
— *Kabir*, The Kabir Book, *translated by Robert Bly*

*It has happened during the last years (and from this I
come by degrees to believe in miracles) that I have been
able to sit down at a meal without computing the calories
involved, without warning my appetite about its excess,
without fearing what might happen if I took pleasure
from my plate. My body, my hunger and the food I give
to myself, which have seemed like enemies to me, have
now begun to look like friends. And this, it strikes me, is
the way it should be; a natural relationship to oneself
and the food that nourishes one.*

— *Kim Chernin*

CHAPTER TEN

Making Daily Inventories And Amends

*Continued to take personal inventory and when we were wrong, promptly admitted it.**

The Tenth Step marks an important transition point for those of us journeying on the Twelve Step path of recovery. Until now, each Step served to prepare us for a new way of life—a new consciousness. This Step is given as a daily practice that will further our transformation through the rest of our lives.

When I reached this transition point I looked back over the months I had been working the Steps. Almost two years had passed since I had first come into Overeaters Anonymous and admitted my powerlessness over my eating. I had avoided the spiritual aspects of the program for six or seven months and had tried to use OA as a diet club, going to meetings for support while trying to control my eating with a food plan. Only when it became obvious that OA was not going to help so long as controlling my food intake was my only

---

* Step Ten, the Twelve Steps of Overeaters Anonymous, adapted from the Twelve Steps of Alcoholics Anonymous. The complete Twelve Steps of AA appear on page 221.

goal was I willing to explore the strange group of Steps urging me toward finding a God I did not believe in.

Along the way, I identified the inner and outer expressions of my egocentricity, and noted those elements of my psyche that were blocking the establishment and maintenance of conscious contact with my inner source of power and wisdom. As I practiced non-judgmental awareness and self-forgiveness, I slowly developed the capacity to choose, to act contrary to the impulses of my ego-mind. As the motivating force of my actions became more centered in my Higher Power and less in my need to shore up and protect my ego-mind, impatience was slowly replaced by patience, dissatisfaction by acceptance, while fear was being transformed into love and compassion. These changes were further deepened by acknowledging the harm I had caused others in the past as a result of acting out of my character defects, and by taking the necessary steps to rectify matters. By the time I was making my amends, dramatic changes had occurred in my outlook and personality. And I had not eaten compulsively during this period of time.

Despite all the incontrovertible changes that had taken place in my attitudes, emotions, and behaviors, however, I remained skeptical about whether this Twelve Step process could really bring about profound, long-lasting changes. *Maybe these changes are just temporary*, I thought to myself frequently. Each time I passed up an opportunity to binge I was incredulous. It remained hard for me to believe that I could be tired or bored and not eat over it, or that I could see food on a buffet table at a party and not overindulge. And when someone irritated me by not behaving as I wanted, I surprised myself by responding by either walking away or addressing the person evenly without anger in my voice.

My ego-mind fought hard to prevent me from accepting the obvious fact that I was more relaxed in social interactions and less afraid of the future, and that the lifelong burdens of guilt, shame, and buried resentments were lifting. That part of me still tried to deny what even my friends and family noticed, that I had become less interested in trying to change people and situations beyond my control, and that I was more capable of maintaining a sober and balanced attitude in the midst of crisis and hardship.

Steps Ten through Twelve are often referred to as the *Maintenance Steps*. When we have sufficiently resolved issues from our past, we are ready to incorporate daily practices that become the foundation for a moral or spiritual life. This does not mean that what we have done and learned up to now is complete and can be abandoned. As we shall see, especially in our discussion of Step Twelve, the principles and practices established in the earlier Steps are woven back into the tapestry of our daily life as we make the Maintenance Steps the basis for sober living. The Twelve and Twelve puts it this way: ". . . when we approach Step Ten we commence to put our A.A. way of living to practical use, day by day, in fair weather or foul. Then comes the acid test: can we stay sober, keep in emotional balance, and live to good purpose under all conditions?"[1]

The first of these Maintenance Steps directs us to take a regular personal inventory and promptly admit our mistakes where we have acted in unskillful ways. We must practice "unsparing self-survey and criticism. For the wise have always known that no one can make much of his life until self-searching becomes a regular habit, until he is able to admit and accept what he finds, and until he patiently and persistently tries to correct what is wrong."[2] This idea is reflected in a story from the *Zohar*, the thirteenth century book of Jewish mysticism. Sitting by the gate of Lydda, the wise and kindly Rabbi Abba sees an old man walking up the road toward the city. The traveller moves slowly along the path, obviously tired after what must have been a long day's journey. Before arriving at the town gate, the old man leaves the road to take shelter under a shady tree and prepare a place to sleep for the night. As Rabbi Abba watches the old man sleeping he notices that the tree and the old man are both settled at the edge of a high precipice.

Suddenly, a poisonous snake comes crawling toward the sleeping man and prepares to strike. Before the Rabbi has a chance to cry out a warning, a large branch falls from the tree, crushing the snake. The old man, startled by the noise of the falling branch, wakes with a start. Seeing a poisonous snake next to him, he immediately jumps up and away from his resting place. At that moment, the ledge breaks away in the exact spot where the man had been quietly sleeping and crashes down the mountainside. It is obvious to the Rabbi that had the old man awakened any later, he would surely have fallen to his death. The Rabbi is amazed at what he has just witnessed and rushes to the man, asking him in astonishment, "Who are you, old man, that God should perform not one but two miracles for you, one after the other?" The reply comes. "I am no one special."

But the Rabbi presses him for more information, determined to discover the secret of this man's special favor in the eyes of the Lord. Pondering the Rabbi's question for a while, the man finally answers, "The only thing I can think of is that I have always made it a habit that if anyone wrongs me in any way, I always try to forgive him at once and make my peace. If, at the end of the day, I find I am still upset with someone, I can't sleep until I forgive him in my heart." Rabbi Abba looks at the man with tears in his eyes and says, "It is no wonder God performs miracles for you."

I have kept a journal since beginning my Step work, and when I began working Step Ten, I found the journal an excellent place to write my daily inventories. Each evening, before going to sleep, I would take a few moments and reflect on my day, noting significant instances in which my character defects might have motivated my actions. Following the suggestions in the Big Book I would ask myself the following questions as I wrote: Was I impatient or intolerant of others? Did I act out of anger or frustration? Were there moments in which I treated others with disrespect or unkindness? What thoughts fostered my self-pity and dissatisfaction?

To avoid the tendency toward self-condemnation and to maintain a balanced perspective, some people suggest including a list of positive actions in the inventory. I have found it more helpful to preserve the function of the inventory as a vehicle for identifying expressions of egocentricity. It is not a vehicle for self-esteem building. I examine my actions as skillful or unskillful, rather than good or bad. I do not use what I observe as a basis for evaluating myself. For me, spiritual recovery is about awareness and compassion, not self-evaluation. Naturally, there are times when I feel self-critical or impatient with myself. In these moments, the words of the Big Book often provide comfort, reminding me that I do not have to be perfect: "We have entered the world of the Spirit. Our next function is to grow in understanding and effectiveness. This is not an overnight matter. It should continue for our lifetime."[3]

Some evenings, I do uncover disturbing aspects of myself that were expressed in my unskillful actions during the day. My mind immediately wants to engage in self-condemnation. The Big Book addresses this tendency of the mind and offers the following help:

> But we must be careful not to drift into worry, remorse or morbid reflection, for that would diminish our usefulness to others. After making our review we ask God's forgiveness and inquire what corrective measures should be taken.[4]

Journal writing done regularly helps me identify and reflect on the attitudes and beliefs underlying my anger, self-pity, and fear. By daily writing about these matters, I minimize the possibility that resentment, guilt, and fear will build up in my psyche. So often in the past when I was angry at someone, the incident and my anger would slip from consciousness.

Days later, when I would see my offender, feelings of anger and tension would arise that I would express in my tone of voice or through some element of withholding on my part. My manner would then cause a reaction in the other person that would trigger a new round of unpleasantness and resentment. If the fragments of these events and reactions are allowed to slip quietly from awareness, they fester below our surface consciousness and diminish our sense of freedom, spontaneity, and capacity for compassion and kindness.

Writing an evening inventory brings the little resentments and unfinished business of the day into awareness, enabling me to bring some closure to those situations. If I discover the need to make amends to someone for something I said or did, I commit myself, in writing, to taking care of it as soon as possible. In other situations, I uncover resentment toward others for something they have done to me. I then have a chance to investigate the roots of my feelings and to decide what actions, if any, are appropriate. I might find upon self-examination and identification that my own rigid demands and expectations are the source of my resentments, in which case the best approach might be to do inner work with these feelings. Or it may become clear to me that the other person has been in some way abusive to me or has violated my boundaries. If so, I note the need to say something to that person, reminding myself that this person was doing the best he or she could under the circumstances. Remembering the story of the boatman and the empty boat, I try to distinguish the actor from the action.

Sometimes, I realize I can't talk to the person without anger and self-righteousness. When I find that to be the case, even though I have resolved to say something to the person, I take a period of time for necessary inner work before I attempt to communicate my feelings. Just as I have learned to do with food, I realize I must allow space between my impulse to act and taking action. I cannot expect to improve the situation, whatever it is, by acting impulsively from whatever emotion happens to be my immediate response. So, if I am feeling anger and resentment, I might undertake a period of quiet meditation and self-examination regarding my character defects before taking outward action.

Engaging in regular self-examination helps me keep in mind that my difficulties are only partially inherent in the external situation. No matter what is going on in the world around me, my distress and anxiety result, for the most part, from my unwillingness or inability to accept the limits of my power in the situation.

Recovery is really about maturation—growing up and learning to accept life as it is, not as I wish it to be. To become a fully functioning, effective adult, I have had to learn to live comfortably with the limits of my power to control other people and external events. This has meant that I had to recognize that even my own emotions and thoughts are often beyond my control, that my mind has a "mind" of its own. Paradoxically, my ability to accept that I cannot control outer events or even my own thoughts and emotions has brought changes in all of these areas.

Just as my slips with food have become indicators that I need to examine what is going on inside, when I notice that I am resentful or fearful over some possible future event, I remind myself that I have some soul-searching to do. Both food slips and emotional slips give rise to opportunities for moving forward in my recovery work. I follow similar guidelines with both. First, of course, I must admit that the slip has occurred. But I need to make this admission in a spirit of loving kindness and mercy; otherwise, it is not a good idea for me engage in a close examination of the psychic forces behind it. When I attempt such an inquiry without the benefit of those healing qualities, I find only more self-loathing and suffering. Where I cannot find mercy for myself, I call upon the healing of self-forgiveness by praying to my Higher Power. Then, rather than wallow in self-recrimination, I identify the measures necessary and appropriate to ameliorate any harm I might have done and commit myself to take the necessary actions at my first opportunity. Finally, I carry out those actions, even though they are often wildly opposed by my ego-mind.

Parenting an adolescent is a marvelous vehicle for working on one's character defects. Often, my son and I would battle over some issue that seemed important to each of us at the time, only to end our fight in mutual exhaustion and frustration. At those times we would withdraw, each feeling hurt and misunderstood. And powerless. That was the natural course of our fights over curfews, room cleaning, homework, and all the other battlefields on which the Great War of the Generations is fought in our time and culture.

Sometimes, however, things would go differently. Occasionally, in the middle of one of these futile arguments, I would recognize how hard I was working to make my son be other than who he was, and how appropriate and natural it was for him to resist such efforts. When I had this kind of clarity, events would begin to slow down—almost like a film being run in slow motion. Suddenly, there was time and opportunity to witness our father-son drama as just that—a drama, a universal human expression of what fathers and sons do. Nothing personal. And in that moment there would be room to relax, to breathe more deeply and slowly. In the midst of my preaching to him about his offensive behavior and his insistence that I was unfair and unreasonable, I would feel myself letting go. I understood that he was simply doing "adolescent-fighting-for-his-right-to-be-his-own-man," and I was responding with "righteous-father-informing-his-son-on-the-proper-way-to-be." Suddenly, it would all cease to be necessary, and in that moment something new was free to happen.

Sometimes, in those moments of lucidity, I would simply inform my son that I no longer wished to play the game and walk away. On one occasion, I was startled to hear myself say something like, "It sure is weird sometimes, doing this father-son thing." We both softened and smiled; in that moment all the walls between us came down. I laughed and speculated aloud to him, "Who knows. Maybe if people really do reincarnate, you will have to be the father next time, and I'll get to be the son." We gave that possibility a quick reflection, each of us certain he would get the better deal under those conditions. The anger and tension that had marked our encounter dissolved into respect and tenderness. I still wanted him to change his behavior, and he still wanted me off his back, but instead of fear and anger, we experienced the deep, pure love we each feel for the other.

In addition to writing evening inventories, as part of my Tenth Step work I have incorporated a practice from the Buddhist tradition called *bare attention or mindfulness*.[5] I endeavor to maintain full consciousness through non-judgmental awareness from my first waking moments: while brushing my teeth, during the Yoga exercises that I do each morning, in my breakfast conversation with my wife, and so on throughout the day. I am rarely able to remain truly mindful for more than a few moments at a time. Sometimes days go by and I do not remember the practice.

When I first began working with this practice, the only thing I got from it was the shocking discovery of how small a percentage of time I am actually conscious of what is going on. I saw that my days were one long daydream. I noticed how often I would arrive home after leaving work, only to realize that I had no recollection of anything that occurred during the drive. I was shocked to discover that I would eat meal after meal without any awareness of what or how I was eating or how the food tasted. As long as I stayed trapped in my limited ego consciousness, I was defenseless against the impulse to eat and similarly remained oblivious to all but a fraction of my sensory world. To the degree that I was thus unconscious, I was at the mercy of thoughts and emotions continuously arising and floating away within me. With discipline, however, I slowly developed the capacity to remain conscious for longer and longer periods of time.

By practicing the discipline of bare attention around mealtime, I slowly grew in my ability to attend to what and how I was eating. For instance, I became able to track the speed with which I ate and could chose to slow down the pace. I had never been able to use the tips suggested by behavioral modification proponents because once I started eating, I could never remain conscious enough to *remember* to use them. However, working with the discipline of bare attention, I was able to remind myself to set down my fork and stop eating periodically. Then, in the moments of non-action, I could note my level of hunger and check for signs of anxiety or tension—the sensations that I most often associated with the need to continue eating.

Practicing mindfulness at other times during the day also proved beneficial. It takes persistent but gentle practice to simply notice the appearance of emotions like frustration, boredom, and fear as they arise and dissolve, rather than acting on them impulsively, without awareness. In the early stages of my practice, for example, I rarely paid attention to feelings of irritation until they became quite strong. When buried feelings of irritation burst into consciousness, I would act out my anger in ways inappropriate to the situation. By the time I realized what was happening, I could only watch and experience the painful events that by then were moving beyond my control like a boulder careening down a mountainside, crashing into other boulders until there was a devastating avalanche.

Emotional and food binges are similar unconscious activities. Both can begin slowly and imperceptibly, long before anything dramatic happens, in moments of inattention. A seemingly random thought arises in the mind suggesting that on this particular occasion, I can give in to my impulse to eat and still retain the capacity to stop without entering the familiar binge cycle. One can speculate that some small event or aspect of my present circumstance might have triggered enough discomfort to generate that thought as a conditioned neural response. We could say it is one of a number of recurring thoughts that arise out of the sea of thoughts that continuously ebb and flow through my mind. For some unfathomable reason, in this particular moment I am vulnerable.

Whatever their source, thoughts of food and eating almost always found me unprotected in the past. They arose and I ate and that was that. Now, when such thoughts arise I do not act on them, and only rarely do I have to exercise conscious will to resist the temptation. If I had to rely on my willpower, without the benefit of my spiritual resources, I am certain that sooner or later it would fail me and I would return to compulsive eating.

What allows me freedom and flexibility in my responses to life is the awareness that the source of my trouble is within me, not out in the world. In the past, I always assumed that my vulnerability was the result of external circumstances. The food on the table or in the bakery window called to me like the Sirens calling Odysseus and his sailors, and I was powerless to avoid succumbing to their song. In recovery, I have learned that the voices trying to draw me off course are within me, and what gives them much of their power is my failure to recognize that fact. So long as I project my impulses and motivations outward on to other people and inanimate objects, I remain powerless to choose my course of action—to be responsible, mature.

The myth of Odysseus, like all the great myths, speaks to us about our inner nature—our psychic life. The Sirens represent psychic forces that are within us, as do the evil witches, powerful dragons, and foolish kings in the fairy tales told us as youngsters, which we then pass on to our own children. When we begin to recognize the things, events, and images that insistently reappear in the course of our destructive behaviors as symbols of the dark forces of our own psyches, we can develop strategies for our spiritual transformation.

My emotional binges are almost always triggered by some external event. Someone makes a comment I do not like, or cuts in front of me in a long line where I have been waiting impatiently for my turn. In one moment I am quiet, floating in some memory or fantasy; in the next my ego-mind says I have been wronged and, without a moment's reflection, I react. Whether I say something hostile or merely steam inside, the result is the same for me—I feel tense and irritable. Sometimes I indulge in an internal monologue of self-pity, complaining about having to relate constantly to flawed human beings. Whatever form my reaction takes, if I do not attend to it, it will provide the foundation for what will eventually become a major binge—emotional or gustatory.

After several years in recovery I still experience occasional slips with both food and emotions. There have been times when I've eaten more than necessary for my physical requirements, sometimes taking second helpings when the voice of reason advises that I should declare the meal over and leave the table. However, since I began working the Twelve Steps, I have not found it necessary to binge on food; I have not entered that awful cycle that always ends in shame and demoralization.

Emotional bingeing, however, has not disappeared from my life. I still get angry sometimes when others don't see things my way. I still experience irritation when things turn out to be more complicated or difficult than I had expected. But now I am much less likely to act out my anger by resorting to verbal abusiveness or long periods of hostile sulking. I am gaining in maturity, learning to tolerate disappointment and frustration when I don't get things my way. When these feelings arise, I now have the capacity to consider my options and choose an appropriate course of action. Sometimes, I decide simply to walk away from the situation and let it go. Other times, it seems more appropriate to discuss my feelings and wants with the other person. When I do choose this alternative, I remind myself that *I am responsible for my feelings,* not the other person. At the same time, *I am responsible for deciding whether to tell someone how I am feeling in response to their behavior or let it go.* In knowing which I need to do in more and more situations, I have been able to mature and establish and maintain healthier relationships.

Avoiding extremes; practicing attention and adjustment rather than denial and resistance; seeing food and my emotions and thoughts as the materials with which I practice—these are ways I am learning I needn't live in fear of the things that once controlled my life. I've begun cultivating an attitude of friendliness toward those things in life I've feared and resisted. Of course, this friendliness can't become a license to act without consideration for the consequences of my choices. I remain mindful of my vulnerability to the prompting of my addict-mind, and remember it will always attempt to draw me into the misuse of my emotions and food. But to the extent I've developed a respectful, yet shame- and fear-free relationship to whatever my mind, to what *life* puts before me, I've found peace and serenity. Krishnamurti said:

> *It is not that you must be free from fear; the moment you try to free yourself from fear you create a resistance against fear. Resistance in any form does not end fear. What is needed rather than running away, or controlling, or suppressing or any other resistance is understanding fear. That means watch it. Learn about it. Come directly into contact with it. We are to learn about fear, not how to escape from it nor how to resist it through courage and so on.*[6]

As long as I fear food, fat, and hunger, I will remain prisoner to the insanity of my addictive thinking. If I continue to act out of fear, sooner or later I will be driven back to compulsive eating. If I perceive food to be a dangerous enemy to be crushed, I will remain at the very level of consciousness that perpetuates the tension and suffering my addictive behavior was an attempt to ameliorate. Fear will not lead me to freedom; only an open investigation of my fear can bring about the liberation I seek.

Like many people, I developed a thick, hard crust around my spirit in response to the hardships of childhood. As I grew older, I continued to rely on the defenses I had established to protect me from further harm. But the very defenses I developed prevented me from recovering that inner source of spiritual power. I spent years looking outside myself for something that could alter my feelings about myself and life, certain that if only some wonderful person would come along and love me unconditionally, I could find happiness; or that if only I had this material possession or could live in those circumstances or ingest so much of that food, I might find peace. But no substance, person, material object, or activity could heal my wound and restore my sense of wholeness.

I now understand that nothing *out there* could make the difference because the emptiness, the longing, is for something within my own heart. The Steps have led me inward, and for the first time in my life I've experienced periods of profound inner peace; I'm experiencing the promises of the program from the discussion of Step Nine in the Big Book. The promise of the Tenth Step, that my obsession to eat compulsively would be lifted, is being fulfilled.

Recall that the Ninth Step promised changes in attitude and personality—one would perceive things in a new way and respond differently to life's inevitable difficulties. Because we experience ourselves and events with more patience, humility, and ease, we act with less hostility, fear, and need to control others. We feel differently about ourselves, and others notice that we are different. The promise of Step Ten is of a different order in that it relates specifically to the lifting of the *obsession* to drink (or compulsively overeat). In the discussion of what happens to the alcoholic at this stage in recovery, a startling promise is made: the obsession to drink alcohol will be lifted from the alcoholic's thinking. The Big Book does not promise that a spiritual awakening will restore one's ability to control when, if, or how much one drinks; the alcoholic is promised that the obsession to drink will be removed, and any occasional temptation to drink will be resisted.

To understand the full impact of this promise, it is necessary to remember that there are two thoughts that work together to produce a compulsive action. If either is not present, one is free to choose his or her behavior. The *first thought* is the impulse—the instantaneous recall of the substance or act we automatically associate with relief from disease and discontent. The *second thought* is the belief, however formulated, that to act on the impulse will bring the peace, joy, or comfort we yearn for without harmful consequences, our past experiences to the contrary. An obsession sufficient for us to act involves both the thought of action and the thought that, this time, our life will be transformed from hell to heaven by taking the action.

The alcoholic is not promised that the impulse to drink will be completely removed, although for many that is just what happens. For others, the urges do continue, most often appearing during times of stress. The impulse, however, has lost the power to drive the person to act because he or she has been "restored to sanity" and no longer forgets the consequences. The Big Book gives us the following description of this stage of our recovery:

And we have ceased fighting anything or anyone—even alcohol. For by this time sanity will have returned. We will seldom be interested in liquor. If tempted, we recoil from it as from a hot flame. We react sanely and normally, and we will find that this has happened automatically. We will see that our new attitude toward liquor has been given us without any thought or effort on our part. It just comes! That is the miracle of it. We are not fighting it, neither are we avoiding temptation. We feel as though we had been placed in a position of neutrality—safe and protected. We had not

> *even sworn off. Instead, the problem has been removed. It
> does not exist for us. We are neither cocky nor are we afraid.
> This is our experience. That is how we react so long as we
> keep in fit spiritual condition.*[7]

Unless we have been driven by an obsession, we cannot appreciate the enormity of this promise. Those of us who have lived for years under the power of an obsession or compulsion find it hard to imagine ever being free of its influence. It is as though we have been imprisoned in a beast's cave with only enough chain to reach the entrance. When we approach the entrance we see the world outside but cannot imagine ever being free to explore it. Naturally, when we first discover the chain is no longer around our neck, we do not venture out very far for fear the beast will catch us and drag us back into the terrifying darkness. But, by the time many of us reach the Tenth Step, we have discovered that so long as we continue to live by the principles and follow the practices of the Twelve Steps, we need not fear its return.

The obsessive desire for my old binge foods has been lifted, even though urges and impulses still appear from time to time. I occasionally want a second helping of some food I find delicious, and, particularly when I am tired and bored, I want to indulge in late-night snacking. Even though occasionally I allow myself these pleasures, there is none of the former intensity of emotion, none of the inner torment and struggle attached to the act. And when I have enjoyed a reasonable portion of whatever it is, I feel satisfied, at peace. I have not eaten to satisfy "the hunger that food cannot satisfy."[8]

I am aware that what I have just said may disturb many in OA who believe that compulsive overeaters have an allergy to certain foods, just as the alcoholic is said to be allergic to alcohol. For example, some OA members believe that we are allergic to flour and sugar and that we must abstain from eating those substances. It is their experience that to eat these foods is to initiate a round of bingeing. I'm certainly not suggesting that any recovering overeater eat anything he or she has reason to believe will lead to a binge. Just because I've found that I can eat just about every kind of food, I do not wish to suggest that everyone can do the same. If we have learned we cannot limit the amount we eat of certain foods, we are better off abstaining from these foods. I do not appear to have any food allergies, at least in the sense that certain foods cause dramatic physiological changes in my body that lead me to crave large quantities of those foods. In the past, any food would do for a binge—pizza and peanut butter were my favorites—but cabbage and tuna would do if that was what was available when the urge arose.

I stated in Chapter One my belief that the question of whether we have an allergy or not is irrelevant. As my spiritual recovery has deepened, my obsessions—whether with a substance or behavior—no longer have the power they once did. Pizza is just food now and not a solution to any problem other than that of fueling my body for one meal period. OA as a whole does not attempt to advise on these matters. What OA does offer is a process through which I regain—recover—my capacity to make reasonable decisions with regard to eating and the power to follow through on them.

The Tenth Step makes recovery a daily practice, providing a basis for making reasonable decisions and carrying them out in all areas of our lives. We recover our integrity—our ability to decide and act in a manner consistent with our values.

Meditation is not a matter of trying to achieve ecstasy, spiritual bliss or tranquility, nor is it attempting to become a better person. It is simply the creation of space in which we are able to expose and undo our neurotic games, or self-deceptions, or hidden fears and hopes.

— Chogyam Trungpa

Prayer is not asking for things—not even for the best things; it is going where they are. The word, with its inevitable sense and stain of supplication, is therefore best abandoned. It is meditation and contemplation; it is opening another aperture of the mind, using another focus, that is the real recreative process.

— Gerald Heard

All meditation systems either aim for One or Zero— union with God or emptiness. The path to One is through concentration of Him, to the Zero is insight into the voidness of one's mind.

— Joseph Goldstein (quoted by Daniel Goleman)

CHAPTER ELEVEN

Improving Conscious Contact

Sought through prayer and meditation to improve our conscious contact with God as we understood Him, *praying only for knowledge of His will for us and the power to carry that out.**

For many years, food was my Higher Power. It was my companion and comforter, and my relationship to it over-shadowed all relationships. Obsessing over my next meal, or feeling remorse over the fact that I had overeaten during my last one, brought my mind to *one-pointed attention*. Most meditation techniques involve focusing the mind on one object and trying to keep it on that point. So, in a sense, my binges had the quality of a meditation—my attention would be withdrawn from other matters and focused solely on the act of putting food into my mouth and swallowing. Thoughts and feelings were subdued, pushed out of consciousness, at least momentarily. During the early moments of the binge, my rambling, troublesome mind was stilled—food and I became one.

Looking back over those years of bingeing, I can see clearly how, like meditation, this activity had as one of its principal

---

* Step Eleven, the Twelve Steps of Overeaters Anonymous, adapted from the Twelve Steps of Alcoholics Anonymous. The complete Twelve Steps of AA appear on page 221.

aims the quieting of my chattering mind. However, while meditation brings us into contact with our spiritual and psychic core, bingeing, like all compulsive behaviors, keeps us *from* our source of wisdom and power. Here, in microcosm, is the human dilemma. We experience a hunger—a craving for something—that we believe can be satisfied by connecting with something outside ourselves. Whether the connection we seek is with a lover, merchandise in a store, alcohol or other drugs, or food, we are hoping to experience a high, that rush of excitement or pleasure. We believe that this time the feeling will last and thus, finally, permanently satisfy our inner hunger. But each time we come down, we are left exhausted and defeated, the ecstasy replaced by despair and anxiety. Like Icarus, flying too near the sun with wings of wax, our wings melt and we are dashed into the sea.

The message is repeated throughout the world's mythological and spiritual teachings—the spiritual yearning within each human being cannot be satisfied other than by establishing and maintaining contact with an inner source of power that provides knowledge of one's true nature. Whether it is called God, Higher Self, One's True Nature, or the Void, it is through turning inward in search of this power that one is transformed and the yearning satisfied.

I came into Overeaters Anonymous conscious only of seeking the answer to how I could lose weight and keep it off. But I harbored a more fundamental question that revealed my true motives and marked me as an addict: how could I learn to control my eating so that I could use food to keep me from feeling bad, without eating so much that I remained overweight? All my life I had been searching for one of two diets. The first would allow me to eat whatever and whenever I wanted and still be thin; the second would restrict my intake sufficiently so that I could remain thin, but without feelings of hunger. By the time I came to OA, I knew the first was impossible, but the second still seemed attainable. I wanted OA to give me a diet that would allow me to live without ever feeling that awful sensation of hunger, because I knew that if I continued to experience that sensation I would not be able to stay within the limits of the diet.

During my journey into recovery, I discovered that so long as I sought satisfaction through food I would never live free from the compulsion. Only when I realized that the hunger I was trying to satisfy was a spiritual one was I able to experience true satisfaction. I have come to accept that sometimes I will be hungry, just as I will be lonely, sad, and all the other sensations and emotions natural to human beings. But I no longer have to eat over those feelings because I have the capacity to observe them without acting on them. Learning to satisfy my spiritual hunger has given me the ability to tolerate discomfort without needing to engage in compulsive behavior.

One of the universal methods for turning inward in quest of spiritual power is prayer and meditation, and in Step Eleven we are invited to make these activities a part of our daily life. Many years before coming to Overeaters Anonymous, I had experimented with various forms of meditation. I took a number of classes in Hatha-Yoga and other meditation techniques from the Hindu tradition, and practiced Zazen and other forms of Buddhist meditation. On the emotional level, the ecstatic nature of Hinduism struck a positive chord in me. My rational mind, however, recoiled from what seemed to me to be the childlike surrender to gurus and multifarious manifestations of God called for in this tradition. I found the non-theistic approach of Buddhism more satisfying intellectually and psychologically and for quite awhile practiced Zen and Insight Meditation. Something was missing for me as well in Buddhism, however, and despite my initial interest in these practices, I gave them up. While I found Insight Meditation powerful, there was a coolness about this path that did not allow expression of the joy I felt was intrinsically part of a complete spiritual practice.

During those years before coming to OA, I had been searching, without knowing it, for some middle path that would lead me inward to my silent spiritual core, while preserving a joyful, passionate reverence for life. I never found what I was searching for and lost at least my conscious interest in spiritual matters long before I entered the program. By the time I came to Overeaters Anonymous I had no particular interest in spiritual investigations of any sort, including meditation.

In addition to suggesting meditation, Step Eleven also speaks about prayer. While I had tried meditation in the past, I could not recall ever engaging in any activity that might be called prayer—except, of course, when I was a small boy and found myself in a frightening situation. I remember getting lost in the woods during a rainstorm when I was about six years old. Huddled under a tree as darkness fell, I prayed for all I was worth, asking God to help my parents find me. There were also numerous childhood prayers in which I made deals with God: "Okay God, if you help me now, I will always believe in you." "If you really exist, God, prove it by not letting anyone find out what I have done."

By early adolescence, I viewed prayer as an activity for weak, cowardly people who were incapable of handling their problems in a mature manner. I felt that I had outgrown the magical belief that if I talked to God, He would make things go the way I wanted. And I was contemptuous of people who went to church and professed to believe that a Divine Force existed in the universe that loved and cared for a few billion people who lived on a tiny speck of matter in a seemingly endless sea of space. I put God and prayer in the same category with Santa Claus and Christmas present lists.

So when I came to Step Eleven, I was willing to try meditating again and began to practice each morning, but prayer did not seem possible for me. I could not make myself talk to my Higher Power as though it were a person who could hear and speak. I would begin the day with a period of about twenty minutes of silent sitting on a meditation bench, observing air as it passed into my body at the tip of my nostrils. Whenever I noticed I was lost in thought, which was almost a constant experience, I brought my attention back to my breath. When thoughts arose telling me I was doing things incorrectly or that meditation was a stupid thing to be doing, I tried to observe these thoughts as if they were leaves floating down a river. Rather than follow them downstream, I noted their passing while keeping my attention focused on the section of the river in front of me.

Staying with this practice was enormously difficult. Feelings like anger, boredom, and sadness kept rising. Sometimes, I could sit through them and they would pass; other times, I broke off the meditations because I became too uncomfortable to continue. Whenever I ended the sittings early, I reminded myself that I had done the best I could for the time—no judgment, no self-criticism.

After several months of regular sitting, I began to notice that my mind grew quieter during my sittings. Perhaps it would be more accurate to say that while thoughts continued to arise in my mind, I could center myself in a quiet inner spot and merely note their passing while I remained comfortable in silence. When I first began to experience this state, as soon as I was in it for a brief time I would take note of it, and my mind would spin into thoughts about what was going on; then I would pass out of the remarkable state of consciousness in which I had momentarily found myself. But as I became more accustomed to this state, I could remain there, even when I became conscious I was in it.

Occasionally, while in this state, I had the strange, unsettling feeling that I was not alone. I can best describe the sense I had as like an enormous silent wave slowly beginning to lift me up. It was exhilarating and terrifying at the same time. I both hoped to continue having this experience and to never encounter it again.

While I cannot say definitively what these experiences are, I believe they can only be described as spiritual experiences, my personal experience of spiritual awe—both frightening and wonderful.

In the beginning of my Twelve Step work, I thought that prayer and meditation should have been introduced earlier in the process. In typical addict fashion, I was already wanting to improve the program by rearranging the Steps. Since all spiritual traditions place emphasis on these practices as a means of altering one's level of consciousness, it seemed to me that the recovery process should start with them. Although I followed the suggestion of my sponsor to take the Steps in order, I secretly harbored the belief that this Step was placed too far along. By the time I reached it, however, I had come to appreciate the wisdom of the founders of AA. I had learned that it was necessary for my spiritual development to go through the stages of ego deflation, decision making, self-examination, confession, and amends making to establish at least some conscious contact with my Higher Power. Then, by Step Eleven, I would be ready to improve that contact through prayer and meditation.

Step Eleven is very specific regarding the content of one's petitions to God, however one understands God. Throughout AA literature, we are told that the purpose of prayer is not to request favors from our Higher Power, but only to ask for guidance and strength and to express gratitude for what one has been given. It is natural for human beings to call out for divine help when terrible events befall us. Almost instinctively a person may cry out, "God help me," upon receiving news that medical tests indicate a malignant tumor. But these cries for divine intervention are not what Step Eleven refers to; these forms of prayer are not undertaken for the purpose of deepening our conscious contact with our Higher Power. This Step directs us to pray only for knowledge of God's will for us and the power to carry that out.

No one is prohibited from engaging in other forms of prayer; we are free to pray any way we wish and for anything we desire. However, if our goal is liberation from the prison of our addictive minds, then our prayers must be requests for guidance and help in our efforts to serve our Higher Self, not for certain events to occur or not occur. If we pray to receive material things or for specific outcomes to events, our motivation is egocentric. Instead, if we expect to move further along on the path of recovery, we pray for the ability to face life on its own terms. We pray for the patience, strength, and wisdom to live fully and lovingly despite the fact that life is uncertain and often painful.

I spoke earlier of the natural human inclination to split the world of experience into "good" and "bad," and how I had come to believe that one's attachment to what appears good and aversion to what appears bad is the root cause of suffering. By the time I'd reached the Eleventh Step, I was convinced that it is this very pattern of thought that we must change if we are to live free of our addictions and compulsions. So long as we feel compelled to call on our Higher Selves to shape events according to our personal preferences, we will remain caught in the web of desires and fears. Seng Ts'an, the Third Chinese Zen Patriarch, said:

> *The Great Way is not difficult*
>   *for those who have no preferences.*
> *When love and hate are both absent*
>   *everything becomes clear and undisguised.*
> *Make the smallest distinction, however*
>   *and heaven and earth are set infinitely apart.*
> *If you wish to see the truth*
>   *then hold no opinions for or against anything.*
> *To set up what you like against what you dislike*
>   *is the disease of the mind.*
> *When the deep meaning of things is not understood*
>   *the mind's essential peace is disturbed to no avail.*[1]

The *Bhagavad Gita,* one of the principal scriptures of the Hindu faith, stresses that one must distinguish spiritual work which seeks to control events and that which seeks only liberation from egocentric thinking.[2] The *Gita* describes four kinds of spiritual devotees. The first type are those who ask that their suffering be removed. The second type are those who ask for money and material goods. The third type are those who seek liberation or release from the bondage of self or egocentricity. The fourth type, whom the *Gita* describes as practicing the highest form of spiritual devotion, ask nothing of God but to be able to do His will.

Having found a spiritual power within has not guaranteed me freedom from sorrow and grief. Still, because I have developed a connection with my Higher Power, I can choose my response to the pain and sorrow that does enter my life. I am free to respond to adversity in the manner of the couple railing against their fate outside their flooded house in the Sierra foothills, or from the stance of serenity and acceptance demonstrated by the remarkable old man sitting in his truck with the floodwaters all around him.

Harold Kushner describes the use of prayer in his book, *When Bad Things Happen to Good People.* I found the following comments particularly helpful in understanding the nature of prayer:

> We cannot pray that [God] make our lives free of problems; this won't happen, and it's probably just as well. We can't ask Him to make us and those we love immune to disease, because He can't do that. We can't ask Him to weave a magic spell around us so that bad things will only happen to other people, and never to us. People who pray for themselves usually don't get miracles, any more than children who pray for bicycles, good grades or boyfriends get them as a result of praying. But people who pray for courage, for strength to bear the unbearable, for the grace to remember what they have left instead of what they have lost, very often find their prayers answered. They discover that they have more

strength, more courage than they ever knew themselves to have.[3]

My only disagreement with Kushner is his comment that one *cannot* pray in certain ways. As I have said earlier, I think people are free to pray in any way they wish. For those who conceive of God as a projection of a good father, stern grandfather, or a mother figure who answers prayers, it may be appropriate to ask their vision of God for the things they feel they need. After all, this form of prayer does involve faith and surrender and, as such, may be transformative for those who engage in it. Nevertheless, praying in this manner raises obvious problems because, sooner or later, those kinds of prayers are not answered, at least the way we want them answered. If one's faith in God rests on demonstrations of divine intervention in human affairs, will such faith fail when tragedy strikes?

As I have indicated earlier, during my years in OA I have heard many recovering compulsive overeaters describe how they regularly prayed to God for thinness, the strength to resist certain foods, and various improvements in their life circumstances. Unfortunately, when things didn't go so well, they experienced a relapse into compulsive overeating. When things didn't turn out the way they had hoped, they felt betrayed by their Higher Power. Some, with a sense of bitter disappointment, left the program.

When we think of our Higher Power as someone or something to fix us, we are unable to view a relapse as an opportunity to further our spiritual work. If we open ourselves to the changes that our *relationship* with our Higher Power brings, we can treat relapse as a message signaling our need to move beyond a dependency relationship with our Higher Power toward one of co-creation.

As we progress in recovery, our spiritual goals can shift from being taken care of by a transcendent Supreme Being to becoming fully actualized human beings. As such, we become capable of expressing in our everyday actions the most noble and responsible motives of which humans are capable. This is possible when Individuation (Jung's term for self-actualization or spiritual maturation) and psychic wholeness are the goals of our spiritual work. Self-actualization is a spiritual experience rather than a matter of acquiring as many material and experiential toys as possible. Self-actualization is not about doing whatever one desires, buying whatever product pleases the senses, putting one's own wants above the needs and wishes of others. Rather, it is a lifelong process of identifying the deepest urges within us and bringing them into expression through our choices and actions.

As I came to terms with Step Eleven I found it necessary to address the subject of *intuition*. I had always associated the term with lucky guessing or some kind of mysterious sixth sense that seemed to be the province of women. I have come to a new understanding about this way of knowing for which there is so little support in our culture. A significant reference to intuition in the Big Book has helped me tremendously. It is preceded by the suggestion that we begin each day with a morning meditation during which we ask God to direct our thinking and motivation. It continues:

> *In thinking about our day we may face indecision. We may not be able to determine which course to take. Here we ask God for inspiration, an intuitive thought or a decision. We relax and take it easy. We don't struggle. We are often surprised when the right answers come after we have tried this for a while. What used to be the hunch or the occasional inspiration gradually becomes a working part of the mind.*[4]

The more I worked the Steps, particularly daily prayer and meditation, the more comfortable I became relying on my intuition. But I remained uncomfortable with the whole idea for quite a while. It seemed unscientific and irrational and therefore suspect. And yet, I wanted to know more about this concept and to find some guidance. I naturally looked to the works of men and women from my field, psychology. As had often happened, the person whose work most illuminated my thinking was Carl Jung. Once again I uncovered a link between his thought and my experiences in recovery.

Early in his professional life, Jung wrote that human personality and behavior could be understood in terms of four distinct functions—thinking, feeling, sensation, and intuition. The *thinking function* refers to intellectual cognition and forming logical conclusions, and includes objective judgments. This function is like a computer, devoid of emotion and sentimentality. The *feeling function*, for Jung, does not refer to emotional reactions but rather to the process of valuation or subjective judgment. Thinking and feeling functions can thus be seen as two opposite ways of organizing experience. A person who operates from the thinking function says, "I know that is true because it fits the facts and my experience. It is logical." This response often seems cold and rigid to a person who favors the feeling function, who is more likely to express a judgment by saying, "I can't give you a good reason why I think that, it just feels true." To a person who operates exclusively from the thinking function, such a statement is likely to seem shocking in its lack of precision.

In addition to the two judging functions there are two perception functions—sensation and intuition. The *sensation function* includes all perceptions formed by the sense organs, while the *intuition function* is knowledge that is dependent on the unconscious without direct reference to the senses. Our eyes (sensation) tell us about the trees and clouds, while our dreams and imaginings (intuition) describe realities that are beyond our sense's ability to encounter. On one hand, people who place greater reliance on their senses for their understanding of the world often find the ways of those who place greater reliance on their intuitive function mysterious. On the other hand, those who trust their intuitive function more often find those who rely more exclusively on their senses lacking in creativity.

Jung pointed out that each of us has certain preferred judgment and perception functions. Often, we have been raised in a family and society that do not encourage our particular preferences. For instance, I had always thought of myself as a sensing-feeling type. Never having received support for my intuitive function, either in my family, school, or in the culture at large, I learned to rely almost exclusively on my sensing function. I discounted my intuition and thought skeptically of people I met who kept suggesting that one thing that made my work as a therapist so effective was my ability to intuit the childhood experiences of my patients and the unconscious forces that motivated their conscious thoughts and behaviors.

Clearly, much of my skepticism and resistance to spiritual matters in the early years of my recovery came from the fact that rarely did my direct sensory experience or rational thinking satisfactorily reveal spiritual truth. Because I had limited myself to those two faculties for my experience and understanding of the world, I had never taken seriously the idea of exploring the spiritual dimensions of life. It took the crisis with my loss of control over eating to motivate me to take small, measured steps along the spiritual path. Even after progressing well into the Steps, I still often required concrete evidence about everything since it was not in my nature to trust or have faith in non-rational experiences. But eventually, as a result of working the Steps leading up to Step Eleven, I became more willing to trust my intuitive capacities for finding direction and meaning in my life.

In addition to prayer and meditation, I began keeping a dream journal in which I recorded the previous night's dreams and fragments of dreams each morning. Through my dream work, I explored the patterns woven by the images and themes recurring in my dreams that led me to a deeper experience of the workings of my psyche. Like prayer and meditation, this brought me to a more profound experience of my Higher Self. In the words of James Hillman, by "befriending my dreams" I grew spiritually and "through the unconscious, I gain[ed] soul."[5]

Obviously, one's ability to sense and reason is necessary for everyday living in this world. Unfortunately, most of us have come to over-rely on these functions for our experience and knowledge of ourselves and the world around us. Limiting ourselves to these means leaves us with impoverished answers when we contemplate the basic questions, *Who am I?* and *What am I doing here?* As I developed my intuitive capacities, my life was deeply enriched by the new levels my daily experiences took on. Speaking to this point Hillman writes:

> *The gulf between consciousness and the unconscious narrows as we are able to feel for it and give to it, as we are able to live with it as a friend. The continued absorption with one's own inner world leads to experiences within that world, in and for that world. These experiences may have little or no connection with outer life, or with ideational life. That is, they may not immediately lead to a new project or idea, or the solving of a marriage or a job problem. They are experiences about events of one's own life. They are in fact a renewal of the capacity to have experiences, to be an experiencing being. Kicks and thrills and the chase for them fade. As the capacity to experience and to love life as it is grows, one needs fewer events because one has more experiences. This growth is growth of the soul. . . .*[6]

By the time I was ready to move on to Step Twelve, I had had direct experience of a consciousness, a reality that underlies the world of ordinary experience. This led me to a new understanding that I felt I could rightly call a spiritual awakening. However, despite these spiritual experiences, I still spend most of my waking time in a world not apparently changed by the truths they brought home to me.

* * *

Working with the spiritual tools of the Twelve Steps, including prayerful meditation in the Eleventh, does not alter my external world but allows me to see that world with new eyes. I am more capable of understanding other people and their motivations by being more intimate with my thoughts and feelings, and so feel less fearful, more open-hearted. I am finding new purpose and meaning in my life through reliance on my relationship with my Higher Power. I am learning to live in greater harmony with the rest of the world as I continue to uncover an underlying unity and wholeness in my life. I am coming to know and am guided by a personal experience of the ultimate reality that goes by many names.

In T. S. Eliot's poem "East Coker" from *Four Quartets*, there is a profound and beautiful statement that conveys what for me is the essence of Step Eleven.

> *I said to my soul, be still, and wait without hope*
> *For hope would be hope for the wrong thing; wait without love*
> *For love would be love of the wrong thing; there is yet faith*
> *But the faith and the love and the hope are all in the waiting.*
> *Wait without thought, for you are not yet ready for thought:*
> *So the darkness shall be the light, and the stillness the dancing.*[7]

We cannot escape the events and occurrences of life and their essentially unsatisfactory nature. We never get permanent satisfaction, we never get the unconditional love we seek, we never get the body we want that will stand the effects of time. The only solution is to dissolve the organ of suffering itself, which . . . is the idea of an ego to be preserved, committed to its own compelling concepts of what is good and what is evil, true and false, right and wrong. . . .

— *Joseph Campbell*

To the extent that we ourselves are free of suffering, our very being becomes an environment in which others can be free of theirs, if it is the way of things.

— *Stephen Levine*

I now think that for the healer this voyage [of personal growth] means a more or less constant progress on the simultaneously painful and joyful task of self-awareness and self-development, as well as a commitment to a mission of service.

— *Jeanne Achterberg*

CHAPTER TWELVE

Practicing the Principles And Carrying the Message

Having had a spiritual awakening as the result of these steps, we tried to carry this message to compulsive overeaters and to practice these principles in all our affairs.*

The message of the Twelfth Step is simply that, as a result of having worked our way through the preceding Eleven Steps, and of continuing to work the Steps on a daily basis, we have experienced a transformation of personality. This has freed us from the mental obsession that compelled us to engage in our addictive/compulsive behavior. As a natural result of this, we now become willing to carry the message of how we came to this awakening to others who still suffer from the same compulsion or addiction.

The recurring theme throughout this book has been my attempt to come to terms with what this *spiritual awakening* or experience is. Since now in Step Twelve we finally come to a specific reference to this term, we'll delve more deeply into what the experience is that is the primary objective behind

---

* Step Twelve, the Twelve Steps of Overeaters Anonymous, adapted from the Twelve Steps of Alcoholics Anonymous. The complete Twelve Steps of AA appear on page 221.

Twelve Step recovery work—what recovery is about. It is what Dr. Silkworth was referring to in his opinion at the beginning of the book *Alcoholics Anonymous* when he explained that only through experiencing "an entire psychic change" could a true alcoholic hope to live a sane and sober life. This is what he meant when he said of those hopeless alcoholics that

> *once a psychic change has occurred, the very same person who seemed doomed, who had so many problems he despaired of ever solving them, suddenly finds himself easily able to control his desire for alcohol, the only effort necessary being that required to follow a few simple rules.*[1]

Bill W. considered Dr. Silkworth's opinion important. A well-known medical expert in the field of alcohol treatment was acknowledging that despite his extensive medical knowledge and skill, he had often been unable to prevent those who had come through his program from returning to drinking. *It was his opinion that medical science could get problem drinkers sober, but only a radical psychic transformation could keep a true alcoholic sober.* Based on his knowledge and experience of the pioneers of AA, he was of the opinion that a psychospiritual transformation sufficient to reorder the alcoholic's entire life was necessary if the alcoholic was to lead a sane and sober existence.

Dr. Silkworth was not the only eminent man of medicine who thought that only a psychospiritual transformation could save a true alcoholic. Once again Carl Jung enters our discussion. Having made a life study of the psychological nature and significance of spiritual concerns, he concluded that genuine spiritual experiences are authentic, powerful psychic events, capable of shaping human experience. He called these consciousness-altering occurrences *numinosum*. Describing this dramatic and spontaneous type of spiritual experience, Jung wrote:

As far as I have been able to understand it, the phenomenon seems to have to do with an acute state of consciousness, as intensive as it is abstract, a detached consciousness . . . which brings up to consciousness regions of psychic events ordinarily covered with darkness. . . . As a rule, the phenomenon is spontaneous, coming and going of its own initiative. Its effect is astonishing in that it almost always brings about a solution of psychic complications, and thereby frees the inner personality from emotional and intellectual entanglements, creating thus a unity of being which is universally felt as "liberation."[2]

This comment by Jung is interesting in light of his comments to his patient, Roland H. On one hand, Jung made clear that he thought a spiritual experience could and had helped hopeless alcoholics free themselves from the obsession to drink. On the other hand, Jung was rather vague about how Roland might accomplish such a feat. Roland had, after all, been a religious man—a churchgoer. He was encouraged when Jung said Roland might find help in the religious area. But his hopes were "destroyed by the doctor's telling him that while his religious convictions were very good, in his case they did not spell the necessary vital spiritual experience."[3]

Since Jung had suggested that the latter was the only thing that could save him from an agonizing alcoholic death, Roland was desperate to know how he could effect such an experience. Unfortunately, Jung did not have much to suggest, explaining with honesty and humility that he had been trying unsuccessfully to produce the necessary psychic change in Roland through analytic treatment. Whether Jung had specific suggestions or not, Roland, in his recollections as contained in the Big Book, tells us that Jung offered none. Did Jung think spiritual awakenings could be brought about by effort and intention?

Scattered throughout his writings, Jung repeats the sentiments expressed in his introduction to Richard Wilhelm's *The Secret of the Golden Flower*, that a spiritual awakening is usually a spontaneous occurrence, rarely produced by conscious will. However, it is clear that he did believe that in some cases a spiritual experience could be produced in one's psyche. His views to this effect are contained in a letter he wrote to Bill W. during a brief correspondence that took place shortly before Jung died.

In the early 1960s, Bill wrote Jung a letter of acknowledgment and appreciation, describing the latter's influence on the formation of Alcoholics Anonymous. Bill began the letter by reminding Jung of his treatment, years earlier, of Roland H. and the advice to his patient that only a conversion experience could help a chronic alcoholic avoid alcoholic insanity and premature death. He told Jung that Roland eventually had a spiritual awakening by following a plan of action that thereafter became the Twelve Steps of Alcoholics Anonymous. Roland became sober and remained so for the rest of his life, Bill W. explained, through active participation in the AA fellowship. Bill said that Jung's comments to Roland had eventually become "the first foundation stone upon which our Society has since been built."[4]

Bill W. went on to outline the early history of AA, including his own spiritual experience. He told about the subsequent lifting of his alcoholic obsession, which, he suggested, supported Jung's thesis about the power of a spiritual experience to free one from the destructive forces of alcoholism. He then described how, reading William James' *The Varieties of Religious Experience*, he discovered that religious conversion experiences seemed to have a common denominator: *ego collapse at depth*. He explained that Roland must have had such a total ego collapse upon hearing his psychiatrist tell him that he was incurable by all methods known to science. Bill W. compared this to his own darkest moment when Dr. Silkworth told him he was hopelessly doomed to die an alcoholic death, that medicine and science could do no more for him.

In that moment of despair and surrender, Bill abandoned all reliance on reason and will and had what he came to understand as his spiritual experience. Bill concluded his letter by describing how, shortly after his spiritual experience, he had a vision in which he saw a society of recovered alcoholics,

> . . . *each identifying with and transmitting his experience to the next—chain-style. If each sufferer were to carry the news of the scientific hopelessness of alcoholism to each new prospect, he might be able to lay every newcomer wide open to a transforming spiritual experience. This concept proved to be the foundation of such success as Alcoholics Anonymous has since achieved. This has made conversion experiences—nearly every variety reported by James—available on an almost wholesale basis.*[5]

Jung's response to Bill's letter offers a significant link between Jung's work and the ideas and methods of the Twelve Step process. Throughout my recovery experience, I discovered repeatedly how relevant Jung's ideas are to anyone attempting to work the Twelve Step program who is, for whatever reason, unable to respond to traditional Christian notions of a Higher Power. Discovering and reading Jung's letter to Bill W. closed the circle that began with my initial reading of Jung's comments to Roland H. in the Big Book.

Jung began his letter to Wilson by explaining that he had always needed to exercise care in the use of spiritual and religious language in his writings. His caution was necessitated, he explained, by popular misunderstandings and prejudice regarding "religious" terms. Because of that concern he had been judicious in his choice of words, even during his conversation with Roland, for fear of being misunderstood and arousing the man's possible prejudices against formal religious teachings and organizations. Consequently, he had refrained from telling Roland the full nature of his theory of alcoholism and why he thought a vital spiritual experience was essential to successful treatment. Jung then wrote as follows:

> *His craving for alcohol was the equivalent, on a low level, of the spiritual thirst of our being for wholeness; expressed in medieval language: the union with God.*
>
> *How could one formulate such an insight in a language that is not misunderstood in our days?*
>
> *The only right and legitimate way to such an experience is that it happens to you in reality, and it can only happen to you when you walk on a path which leads you to higher understanding. You might be led to that goal by an act of grace or through a personal and honest contact with friends, or through a higher education of the mind beyond the confines of mere rationalism. I see from your letter that Roland H. has chosen the second way, which was under the circumstances, obviously the best one.*[6]

Here is the clearest statement that both men viewed alcoholism as a spiritual problem, a spiritual disorder having emotional and physical symptoms to be sure, but fundamentally an illness of the soul. Each believed, one from his vast experience as a healer and the other as a recovering drunk, that the alcoholic drinks, despite the indisputable evidence that he should not, to ameliorate the psychological and spiritual suffering resulting from the loss of contact between his ego and Higher Self. The obsession to drink grows out of a misguided effort to satisfy what is, in essence, a spiritual thirst. This thirst can only be satisfied by establishing and maintaining contact with the healing power and creative energy deep within the human psyche. All substitutes turn out to be dust in the mouth.

Having investigated why a spiritual awakening is a necessary underpinning to a life of sobriety for an alcoholic, let's turn our attention to the nature of such experiences. We begin our discussion with Bill W.'s description of his own spiritual experience, and then we may begin to draw comparisons to those of others, including myself.

Bill W.'s spiritual experience is described in some detail in his official biography published by Alcoholics Anonymous[7] and is a bit more extensive than is suggested in his letter to Jung. Apparently, in the summer of 1934, Dr. Silkworth told Bill W. that Bill was a hopeless case, that medical science could not keep him from continuing his descent into chronic alcoholism, insanity, and eventual death. As he had considered Dr. Silkworth and his clinic his only hope, Wilson went through a period of deep despair. He continued to drink and remained drunk much of the time.

In November of that year an old drinking buddy of Wilson's, Ebby T., came to visit him. Bill was drunk at the time but not too drunk to notice that his friend had changed. Ebby explained that he no longer drank and had become sober and maintained his sobriety through religion. Wilson reported that while he was intrigued by his friend's success story, he was repelled by the religious approach and the suggestion that one could be helped through a relationship with a personal God. However, in desperation, Wilson began attending meetings of the Oxford Group[8] with Ebby where, incidentally, he met Roland H., who was also sober by this time.

Despite his attendance at the Oxford Group meetings, Bill continued to drink and once again found himself in Dr. Silkworth's clinic. Again, the doctor told Bill that there was nothing he could do but help his patient sober up; he was powerless to prevent Bill from returning to the bottle on the occasion of the first impulse to drink. Sitting alone in his hospital room, Wilson experienced a sense of total despair. Envisioning spending the remainder of his days in a back ward of a mental hospital horrified him. He saw no way out of his predicament. He no longer believed that he could save himself through willpower or the skills of the medical community. The only solution seemed to be through faith in God, and he had no such faith.

> *He had reached a point of total, utter deflation—a state of complete, absolute surrender. With neither faith nor hope, he cried, "If there be a God, let Him show Himself."*
>
> *What happened next was electric. "Suddenly, my room blazed with an indescribably white light. I was seized with an ecstasy beyond description. Every joy I had known was pale by comparison. The light, the ecstasy—I was conscious of nothing else for a time.*
>
> *"Then, seen in the mind's eye, there was a mountain. I stood upon its summit, where a great wind blew. A wind, not of air, but of spirit. In great, clean strength, it blew right through me. Then came the blazing thought 'You are a free man.' I know not at all how long I remained in this state, but finally the light and the ecstasy subsided. I again saw the wall of my room. As I became more quiet, a great peace stole over me, and this was accompanied by a sensation difficult to describe. I became acutely conscious of a Presence which seemed like a veritable sea of living spirit. I lay on the shores of a new world. 'This,' I thought, 'must be the great reality. The God of the preachers.'*
>
> *"Savoring my new world, I remained in this state for a long time. I seemed to be possessed by the absolute, and the curious conviction deepened that no matter how wrong things seemed to be, there could be no question of the ultimate rightness of God's universe. For the first time, I felt that I really belonged. I knew that I was loved and could love in return. I thanked my God, who had given me a glimpse of His absolute self. Even though a pilgrim upon an uncertain highway, I needed to be concerned no more, for I had glimpsed the great beyond."*[9]

Until that moment, no human force had been capable of preventing him from returning to the bottle. And yet, from that day, in December of 1934 until his death on January 24,

1971, Bill W. never took another drink. Before this neither social nor business successes, the love and devotion of his wife, Lois, nor the assistance of Dr. Silkworth and his alcohol treatment program had been able to keep him from taking the first drink that inevitably led to drunkenness. In the days and weeks that followed his spiritual experience, Bill was amazed to find himself not wanting to drink; his desire seemed to have been removed. *What had happened to him? he wanted to know. Was his experience real? Could it keep him from wanting to drink? Had others had similar experiences that transformed their lives?*

As mentioned earlier, in search for answers to these questions, Bill turned to *The Varieties of Religious Experience* by the famous American psychologist William James. James explained that spiritual experiences, whatever their form, almost always come on the heels of some great loss or in the face of some imminent peril. In Bill W.'s case, it was both: losing the illusion that he could stop drinking and the loss of self-esteem that accompanied that discovery; and recognizing that he was already dying of alcoholism.

Here was the theoretical foundation for Step One. Until a person experiences and admits the total inability to control the urge to drink (or eat), the requisite ego deflation cannot take place. This is what is meant in the program by the term *hitting bottom*. It does not refer to having lost one's spouse and family or any other material hardship occasioned by compulsive drinking. It does not occur when the alcoholic realizes that only quitting drinking will stop the destruction of his or her life. It occurs when one comes to the shocking realization that nothing can keep him or her from taking a drink when the urge becomes strong enough.

Many people, inside and outside Twelve Step programs, mistakenly believe that Step One requires anyone working the Steps to admit that he or she is forever powerless over everything in life and, therefore, all decisions must be left to others in the program or to God. Such an interpretation, with its requirement of passivity and the relinquishing of personal responsibility for one's life choices, is unacceptable to many. It was to me, and remains so. However, I have come to understand that my powerlessness with regard to compulsive overeating grew out of my inability to derive strength and direction from the Higher Power within me. It was necessary to admit my powerlessness in order to find a Power greater than that of my limited ego-power. Having experienced the spiritual poverty of total identification with my ego, the goal of my recovery work became that of finding and drawing upon a Power within me that had hitherto been unavailable.

The Steps begin with admitting powerlessness over our compulsion and end with acknowledging that we have had a spiritual awakening. What did Bill W. mean by a spiritual awakening? Did he expect all alcoholics to have the kind of transformative vision he had as a result of working the Steps? Again borrowing from James, Bill explained in the Big Book that there are two principal types of spiritual experiences. Bill's was merely one form: the cataclysmic, rushing forth of latent psychic energy. Jung described the universal characteristics and effect of this type of experience in his commentary on an ancient Taoist text of Chinese yoga, *The Secret of the Golden Flower*. He wrote:

> *The phenomenon itself . . . the vision of light, is an experience common to many mystics, and one that is undoubtedly of the greatest significance because in all times and places it appears as the unconditional thing, which unites in itself the greatest energy and the profoundest meaning. . . . As a rule, the phenomenon is spontaneous, coming and going on its own initiative.*[10]

However, there is another equally powerful form of spiritual experience that does not include visions or instantaneous, dramatic psychic events. In the Second Edition of the Big Book, Bill W. sought to clear up a mistaken impression left in the mind of many by the description in the First

Edition of his illumination experience. Apparently, many coming to AA were confused and disturbed by the fact that few of them were experiencing what Bill had described. He noted that the first printing of the Big Book left with "many readers the impression that these personality changes, or religious experiences, [sufficient to bring about recovery from alcoholism] must be in the nature of sudden and spectacular upheavals."[11] He sought to make clear that not everyone experienced an "immediate and overwhelming 'God-consciousness' followed at once by a vast change in feeling and outlook."[12] Borrowing from William James, Bill W. called the gradual, more common form of spiritual awakening the "educational variety." The dramatic nature of the experience is not of prime importance. Instead, it is the fact that a profound change in one's personality and motivations can occur *over time* through the ongoing process of living according to the spiritual principles set forth in the Twelve Steps.

I have not experienced dazzling visions or sudden upheavals in consciousness. But gradually, day by day, I am coming to trust the inner, intuitive wisdom of my own heart in my personal and professional life. Through daily prayer and meditation, I am comforted in moments of pain and sorrow, and find forgiveness and compassion for myself and others as I continue working my recovery program. It is a slow process. Sometimes I even seem to be retreating, falling back into old patterns of resentment and fear. But my character defects do not have the grip on me that they once had. I am more capable of recognizing their appearance and choosing responses that are more skillful than those prompted by my habitual defenses and attitudes.

Having had a spiritual awakening and experienced a measure of sobriety (the capacity for balanced living), we are directed by Step Twelve to carry the message of our experience to others who suffer. Bill W. put it this way in a letter he wrote in 1942:

> *Our chief responsibility to the newcomer is an adequate*
> *presentation of the program. If he does nothing or argues,*
> *we do nothing but maintain our own sobriety. If he starts*
> *to move ahead, even a little, with an open mind, we then*
> *break our necks to help in every way we can.* [13]

We have transformed our compulsion into compassion. For this is the essence of compassion—opening our hearts to the suffering of others and offering to help if help is wanted. Carrying the message of how we live free from the destructive urges of our compulsion on a daily basis, we offer to guide those who still suffer through the Twelve Step process. If the person to whom we speak wants to take the Steps that we have taken, we are available to help them, careful to avoid trying to fix anyone or force anyone to do what we have done. If they decline our help, our compassion enables us to accept their rejection of our assistance without our feeling the need to close them out of our hearts.

In truth, it is sometimes a challenge for me to maintain balance and goodwill in the face of the denial and resistance of those I seek to help. More and more of the time I am up to the challenge, but not always. There are times when I become impatient and irritated because my need to control, to be right, and to fix others prevents me from accepting that the person I seek to help needs to resist and even to reject what I offer. I find myself in the painful situation of trying to enjoy the fruits of another's progress, wanting them to succeed so that my ego might feed off their success. Here I discover traces of false pride and grandiosity. And in that moment of realization I am free to practice detachment. Through this I am able to continue caring about someone who is suffering, while at the same time letting go of the need to have them be other than who they are.

I am reminded of a time when my inability to detach caused pain to both the other person and myself. One morning I was the principal speaker at a newcomers' meeting. I explained to people who had never been to an OA meeting before what the program had done for me and introduced them to its basic concepts and tools. After the meeting, a young woman approached me and said that she was frightened about getting involved in the program but was excited by what I had to say. She was willing to try OA and asked if I would be willing to help her get started. I agreed.

Over the next few weeks she called fairly frequently. Each time she called, she made critical remarks about the program, forever explaining that she didn't like one thing or another about OA. The meetings were boring; the people said stupid things; everyone was crazy—she was continually raising one challenge after another. I listened attentively each time she called, and when she finished complaining I attempted to meet her objections. I suggested, as gently as possible given my growing irritation, that she might do better to work the program, particularly the Steps, rather than spending her time looking for things to criticize. At the end of each of our conversations, she would thank me for taking the time to talk with her, and we would say good-bye. I would hang up feeling angry but said nothing to indicate my true feelings.

Early one Sunday morning, she called to tell me that she had heard several things at a meeting that really put her off and that she had finally decided OA was not for her. She explained that she was calling merely to thank me for my help and to say good-bye. I was furious. I thought to myself, *This woman is waking me up on a Sunday morning to tell me this after I have spent weeks listening patiently to her complaints.* I began unloading anger and frustration that I had been suppressing for weeks. Behind my fury, however, was the deeper feeling of impotence—I had failed to help this woman who clearly was in great pain over her compulsive eating and body image. I hated facing my own powerlessness. Having gotten that off my chest, I then began pleading with her not to give up on herself, expressing my concern about what might happen to her if she left the program and returned to bingeing and purging. Unmoved by my comments, she told me that she was prepared to take her chances. We said good-bye for the last time, and I hung up the phone. I felt like hell, angry at her and disappointed in myself.

That evening I wrote about the conversation in my Tenth Step inventory, reviewing what had happened, looking for what character defects of mine contributed to my emotions and behavior. I noted my eagerness to succeed, to save this poor person, to be a hero. How clearly I saw that my anger had arisen, not from anything this woman had done but from my frustrated need to affect her. My attachment to the outcome of my efforts was the principal source of my frustration and distress and another painful lesson in letting go.

But sponsorship is not only about learning to detach from results. It is, more importantly, an opportunity to pass the message of the program and the potential of recovery to another fellow sufferer. It is the path of the wounded healer, upon which both the injured and the healer are transformed. Ultimately, the way we help another to sobriety and recovery is not through words but by our total presence. As wounded healers, having been given the gift of recovery, we stand in a unique position to be of service to others who suffer from the same illness. Because we have experienced the painful and humiliating conditions of powerlessness over our compulsion and have found a way out of that hell, we can provide hope and assistance to others searching for the power that can bring about their healing. Because we have been given the gift of healing, we can find no greater joy than serving as midwife for others experiencing psychic and spiritual death and rebirth. And as always we work on ourselves, our own character defects, our own holdings and inability to surrender to what is.

Ram Dass offers wise counsel to those who seek to help others. His comments have guided me both as a sponsor in Overeaters Anonymous and as a therapist in my professional practice. He says:

What you and I can offer other human beings is the loving, spacious presence that allows them the space to come up for air out of the entrapping roles that they are imprisoned in if they choose. We do not have any right to force them to come up. You can't take another person's suffering away, but you can become an environment in which other people can come up for air. . . .

We work on ourselves through the way we live in the world in order to become free of our own suffering in order to be an environment through which other people become free of theirs. It is a gift which we offer back to ourselves.[14]

In addition to suggesting that we carry the message of our recovery to others who suffer, Step Twelve encourages us to continue practicing the principles of all the Steps on a daily basis for the remainder of our life. In so doing, Step Twelve, rather than being the end of our Step journey, proves to be a new beginning. Again, T. S. Eliot sums up my sentiments:

We shall not cease from exploration
And the end of all our exploring
Will be to arrive where we started
And know the place for the first time.[15]

Having come a long way on this path of recovery we are not free to rest. Instead, we rededicate ourselves to this new way of life; we have chosen to make our life, as Mahatma Gandhi called his remarkable life, "an experiment in truth."

Having had a spiritual awakening and being in a position to help others in no way means we have reached perfection or some blissful state. We are now at the vanguard, pushing against our limits and risking comfort and security in our commitment to growth and discovery. For as Victor Frankl put it, "What is to give light must endure burning." At the same time, it is important for us to remain aware of our human limitations. To forget them is to lose our humility; to think we are finished learning and growing is to court disaster.

Very early in the process of recovery, it was explained to me that the qualities necessary for recovery are honesty, open-mindedness, and willingness. I have written this book in the spirit of those three qualities. It is my hope that it will serve as a helpful guide to those who might otherwise have turned away from this truly life-restoring process called the Twelve Steps. May we continue to burn so that our light might guide others.

THE TWELVE STEPS
OF ALCOHOLICS ANONYMOUS*

1. We admitted we were powerless over alcohol—that our lives had become unmanageable.

2. Came to believe that a Power greater than ourselves could restore us to sanity.

3. Made a decision to turn our will and our lives over to the care of God *as we understood Him.*

4. Made a searching and fearless moral inventory of ourselves.

5. Admitted to God, to ourselves, and to another human being the exact nature of our wrongs.

6. Were entirely ready to have God remove all these defects of character.

7. Humbly asked Him to remove our shortcomings.

8. Made a list of all persons we had harmed, and became willing to make amends to them all.

9. Made direct amends to such people wherever possible, except when to do so would injure them or others.

10. Continued to take personal inventory and when we were wrong promptly admitted it.

11. Sought through prayer and meditation to improve our conscious contact with God *as we understood Him,* praying only for knowledge of His will for us and the power to carry that out.

12. Having had a spiritual awakening as the result of these steps, we tried to carry this message to alcoholics, and to practice these principles in all our affairs.

---

* The Twelve Steps of A.A. are taken from *Alcoholics Anonymous,* 3rd ed., published by A.A. World Services, Inc., New York, N.Y., 59–60. Reprinted with permission of A.A. World Services, Inc.

Endnotes

PREFACE

1. *Alcoholics Anonymous*, 3rd ed. (New York: Alcoholics Anonymous World Services, 1976), 564.

Chapter 1: ADMITTING POWERLESSNESS

1. The Big Book is the name used to refer to the principal text of the fellowship of Alcoholics Anonymous, which is titled *Alcoholics Anonymous*. The "Steps" are the Twelve Steps, which are described in the Big Book as the basic actions that lead to recovery from alcoholism.
2. Stanton Peele, *The Meaning of Addiction* (Lexington, Mass.: Heath, 1985) and Herbert Fingarette, *Heavy Drinking* (Berkeley: University of California Press, 1988).
3. Dr. William Silkworth directed the alcohol treatment hospital where Bill Wilson had undergone treatment several times before the formation of Alcoholics Anonymous. He wrote "The Doctor's Opinion," which appears in *Alcoholics Anonymous*, xxiii.
4. *Twelve Steps and Twelve Traditions* (New York: Alcoholics Anonymous World Services, 1981), 21. This book is referred to in the program as the "Twelve and Twelve," the title that will be used throughout this book.

Chapter 2: RESTORING SANITY

1. *Alcoholics Anonymous*, 60.
2. Gregory Bateson, "The Cybernetics of Self: A Theory of Alcoholism," in *Steps to an Ecology of Mind* (New York: Ballantine Books, 1972).
3. Arthur Deikman, M.D., *The Observing Self* (Boston: Beacon Press, 1982), 3.
4. The story of Roland H. and his conversation with Dr. Jung is described in *Alcoholics Anonymous*, 26–28.

5. *Alcoholics Anonymous*, 27.
6. Deikman, *The Observing Self*, 8–9.
7. This theme is discussed in greater detail in Step Three (see Chapter Three, pages 49-66).
8. Hazrat Inayat Khan, *The Unity of Religious Ideals* (New Lebanon, N.Y.: Sufi Order Publications, 1979), 31.
9. *Alcoholics Anonymous*, 46–47.
10. Jacob Needleman, *On the Way to Self Knowledge* (New York: Knopf, 1976), 11.
11. *Alcoholics Anonymous*, 569.
12. Ibid.
13. Ibid., 570.

Chapter 3: MAKING A DECISION

1. *Twelve Steps and Twelve Traditions*, 35.
2. I have changed his name to protect the confidential nature of our relationship.
3. Many of the early AA's had been involved with The Oxford Group, including Roland H., Bill W., and Dr. Bob.
4. Joseph Campbell, *Myths to Live By* (New York: Bantam Books, 1972). See also Campbell's *The Hero with a Thousand Faces* (Princeton, N.J.: Bollingen/Princeton University Press, 1968).
5. Aldous Huxley, *The Perennial Philosophy* (New York: Harper/Colophon Books, 1970).
6. Edward F. Edinger, *Ego and Archetype* (New York: Penguin Books, 1972).
7. Aldous Huxley, *Tomorrow, Tomorrow and Tomorrow* (New York: Signet, 1964), 54.

Chapter 4: WRITING A MORAL INVENTORY

1. The terms *skillful* and *unskillful* come from the Buddhist tradition. I find them more compatible with my developing spiritual understanding and experience than words carrying a heavier moral tone such as *bad* or *sinful*. Later in this book I will talk at length about these concepts, but for now it is sufficient to indicate that skillful thoughts and actions are those that

serve to further one's recovery and to minimize the pain and suffering of one's self and others.

2. Carl Jung quoted in *Alcoholics Anonymous*, 27.
3. The format suggested by my sponsor, which I modified, was developed by Bill B., author of the books *Compulsive Overeaters* and *Maintenance*, both published by CompCare. Bill and I have become friends over the years, and his experiences and ideas have been an important source of guidance and inspiration in developing my own understanding of the Twelve Step process of recovery.
4. Perfectionism, along with the belief that "I am different," are perhaps the two most universal characteristics of the belief system of people who are addicted or otherwise compulsive. In the Twelve Step program, they are often considered together under the title "terminal uniqueness."
5. *Twelve Steps and Twelve Traditions*, 48.
6. Ibid., 50.
7. Fritz Kunkel, *Creation Continues* (New York: Paulist Press, 1987), 28.
8. Ibid.

Chapter 5: SHARING THE MORAL INVENTORY

1. *Alcoholics Anonymous*, 72–73.
2. Given the fact that most individuals take their Fifth Step with their sponsor, it is interesting that the Big Book does not even mention using a sponsor in this manner. And the Twelve and Twelve is rather cautious on this subject, stating that while a sponsor might be the right person to tell, he or she might not be suitable. (See *Twelve Steps and Twelve Traditions*, 61.)
3. *Alcoholics Anonymous*, 63.
4. Ibid., 75–76.
5. Ibid., 75.
6. Abraham Maslow is referred to as the founder of the humanistic psychology movement. His interest in the higher levels of human endeavor and consciousness eventually led him to be-

come a key figure in the early development of transpersonal psychology.

7. For more on the nature of shame and its relationship to addiction and recovery see John Bradshaw, *Healing the Shame that Binds You* (Dearfield Beach, Fla.: Health Communications, 1988). Also, Gershen Kaufman, *Shame: The Power of Caring* (Rochester, Vt.: Schenkman Books, 2nd ed., rev., 1985).

8. *Twelve Steps and Twelve Traditions*, 55.

9. Carl Jung, *The Practice of Psychotherapy*, quoted in Dorothy Berkley Phillips, Elizabeth Boyden Howes, and Lucille M. Nixon, *The Choice is Always Ours* (Wheaton, Ill.: Theosophical Publishing, 1982), 300.

10. We will examine the "wounded healer" concept more fully in Chapter Twelve, but I wish to introduce it here because it helps us to understand the power of the sponsor-sponsee relationship, especially with regard to the Fifth Step.

11. *Centaurs* are mythological figures, half man and half horse, that, among other talents, have the capacity to heal the sick and wounded. They are also immortal.

12. This discussion of the wounded healer and the myth of Chiron comes from a fascinating book about medicine and healing by Larry Dossey, M.D., *Beyond Illness: Discovering the Experience of Health* (Boston: New Science Library, 1984).

Chapter 6: WILLINGNESS AND SELF-FORGIVENESS

1. *Alcoholics Anonymous*, 76.

2. Robert Bly, *A Little Book on the Human Shadow* (San Francisco: Harper & Row, 1988).

3. Arthur Egendorf, *Healing from the War: Trauma and Transformation after Vietnam* (Boston: Shambhala Press, 1987), 249. The author describes his recovery from the emotional devastation he experienced as a result of his participation in the Vietnam War. Much of what Egendorf writes about psychic and spiritual disease and psychic healing are relevant to anyone working with the Twelve Step process. This book is highly recommended.

Chapter 7: HUMBLY ASKING

1. *Alcoholics Anonymous,* 76.
2. *Twelve Steps and Twelve Traditions,* 76.
3. Jung spoke of the *animus* and *anima* as respectively, the masculine and feminine aspects of the psyche. The *animus* is the psychic source of human efforts to control and actively influence the world. The *anima* is the source of the human capacity to yield and surrender to forces larger than oneself. It should be understood that people have both elements within their psyches; this model is not advocacy for the sexist attitude that men should be strong and aggressive while women should be soft and yielding. Rather, it indicates that both forces need to be developed and expressed in men and women. A good introduction to this material are three books by the Jungian, Robert Johnson: *He, She,* and *We.*
4. *Spiritual materialism* is a term referring to efforts at spiritual growth that are in fact motivated by the ego; for instance, practicing modesty to create the impression in others and oneself that one no longer suffers from pridefulness.
5. Plato, Aristotle, Epicurus, and the Stoics and Skeptics are the most notable.
6. *Twelve Steps and Twelve Traditions,* 90.
7. The Buddha taught the Four Noble Truths: (1) The fundamental nature of human experience is suffering; pleasure is only temporary. (2) The cause of suffering can be known; it is the mind's effort to cling to the pleasant and avoid the unpleasant, to attempt to fix experience when the nature of reality is that all things are constantly in a state of flux and change. (3) That one can come to experience life free from suffering. (4) Following the path of the Buddha, the Eightfold Path, is the way to liberation from suffering.

Chapter 8: MAKING A LIST OF AMENDS . . .

1. *Twelve Steps and Twelve Traditions,* 80.
2. Ibid., 77.
3. Ibid., 78.
4. *Alcoholics Anonymous,* xxvi-xxvii.

5. *Twelve Steps and Twelve Traditions,* 79–80.
6. Ibid.
7. Egendorf, *Healing from the War,* 190.

Chapter 9: MAKING AMENDS

1. *Alcoholics Anonymous,* 76.
2. Ibid., 77.
3. Ibid., 83.
4. Ibid., 83–84.
5. Ibid.

Chapter 10:
MAKING DAILY INVENTORIES AND AMENDS

1. *Twelve Steps and Twelve Traditions,* 88.
2. Ibid.
3. *Alcoholics Anonymous,* 84.
4. Ibid., 86.
5. Mindfulness, or bare attention, is the primary practice of Vipassana (insight) Meditation. In brief, *mindfulness* involves keeping attentive to whatever arises in the moment, observing the passing show of experience merely as sensations in the body and thoughts in the mind. When sensations and thoughts are made neutral objects of attention, one may perceive the true nature of things, that is, have a spiritual awakening. See Thich Nhat Hanh, *The Miracle of Mindfulness* (Boston: Beacon Press, 1976). See also Joseph Goldstein and Jack Kornfield, *Seeking the Heart of Wisdom: The Path of Insight Meditation* (Boston: Shambhala Press, 1987).
6. Quoted by Ram Dass during a public talk.
7. *Alcoholics Anonymous,* 84–85.
8. I thank my good friend Elad Levenson for coining this phrase.

Chapter 11: IMPROVING CONSCIOUS CONTACT

1. Seng Ts'an, Third Chinese Zen Patriarch, *Hsin Hsin Ming.* Trans. by Richard B. Clarke.

2. There are a number of excellent translations of the *Gita*. I recommend the one with extensive commentary by Eknath Easwaran, *The Bhagavad Gita For Daily Living*, three volumes (Petaluma, Calif.: Nilgiri Press, 1981).
3. Harold Kushner, *When Bad Things Happen to Good People* (New York: Avon Books, 1985), 125.
4. *Alcoholics Anonymous*, 86–87.
5. James Hillman, *Insearch: Psychology and Religion* (New York: Charles Scribner's Sons, 1967), 64–65.
6. Ibid., 63–64.
7. T. S. Eliot, "East Coker" from *Four Quartets* found in *The Complete Poems and Plays* (New York: Harcourt Brace, 1952), 126–27.

Chapter 12: PRACTICING THE PRINCIPLES AND CARRYING THE MESSAGE

1. *Alcoholics Anonymous*, xxvii.
2. Carl Gustav Jung and Richard Wilhelm, *The Secret of the Golden Flower: A Chinese Book of Life* (New York: Harcourt Brace, 1969), 107.
3. *Alcoholics Anonymous*, 27.
4. Letters between Bill Wilson and Carl Gustav Jung. Reprinted in "Parabola," Vol XII, No. 2 (Summer 1987): 68.
5. Ibid., 70.
6. Ibid., 71.
7. *Pass It On: The Story of Bill Wilson and How the A.A. Message Reached the World* (New York: Alcoholics Anonymous World Services, 1984), 120–21.
8. The Oxford Group was an evangelical offshoot of the Episcopal Church that sought to rekindle the moral values and spiritual teachings of early Christianity. One project they undertook was to bring religion to alcoholics in an effort to keep them sober.
9. *Pass It On*, 121.
10. Jung, *The Secret of the Golden Flower*, 107.
11. *Alcoholics Anonymous*, 569.

12. Ibid.
13. Bill Wilson, *As Bill Sees It* (New York: Alcoholics Anonymous World Services, 1967), 105.
14. Ram Dass, from a talk titled, "Cultivating the Heart of Compassion."
15. T. S. Eliot, "Burnt Norton" from *Four Quartets* found in *The Complete Poems and Plays* (New York: Harcourt Brace 1952), 145.

Select Bibliography

Anonymous. *Alcoholics Anonymous Comes of Age*. New York: Alcoholics Anonymous World Services, 1957.

——. *Alcoholics Anonymous*, 3rd ed. New York: Alcoholics Anonymous World Services, 1976.

——. *Overeaters Anonymous*. Torrance, Calif.: Overeaters Anonymous, 1980.

——. *Twelve Steps and Twelve Traditions*. New York: Alcoholics Anonymous World Services, 1981.

——. *Pass It On: The Story of Bill Wilson and How the A.A. Message Reached The World*. New York: Alcoholics Anonymous World Services, 1984.

Assagioli, Roberto. *Psychosynthesis*. New York: Penguin Books, 1976.

Bill B. *Compulsive Overeater*. Minneapolis: CompCare, 1981.

——. *Maintenance for Compulsive Overeaters*. Minneapolis: Comp-Care, 1986.

Bly, Robert. *A Little Book on the Human Shadow*. San Francisco: Harper & Row, 1988.

Bradshaw, John. *Healing the Shame that Binds You*. Dearfield Beach, Fla.: Health Communications, 1988.

Buber, Martin. *I and Thou*. New York: Charles Scribner's Sons, 1958.

——. *Between Man and Man*. New York: Macmillan, 1965.

Campbell, Joseph. *The Hero with a Thousand Faces*. Princeton, N.J.: Bollingen/Princeton University Press, 1968.

——. *Myths to Live By*. New York: Bantam, 1972.

——, ed. *The Portable Jung*. New York: Viking, 1971.

Chernin, Kim. *The Obsession: Reflections on the Tyranny of Slenderness*. New York: Harper/Colophon Books, 1981.

——. *The Hungry Self: Women, Eating and Identity*. New York: Harper & Row, 1985.

Deikman, Arthur, M.D. *The Observing Self*. Boston: Beacon Press, 1982.

Easwaran, Eknath. *The Bhagavad Gita for Daily Living*. (Three Volumes), Petaluma, Calif.: Nilgiri Press, 1975–1984.

——. *Meditation: An Eight-Point Program*. Petaluma, Calif.: Nilgiri Press, 1978.

——, trans. *The Dhammapada*. Petaluma, Calif.: Nilgiri Press, 1986.

——, trans. *The Upanishads*. Petaluma, Calif.: Nilgiri Press, 1987.

Edinger, Edward F. *Ego and Archetype*. Baltimore: Penguin Books, 1972.

Egendorf, Arthur. *Healing from the War: Trauma and Transformation after Vietnam*. Boston: Shambala, 1987.

Eliot, T.S. *The Complete Poems and Plays*. New York: Harcourt, Brace & World, 1952.

Golas, Thaddeus. *The Lazy Man's Guide to Enlightenment*. New York: Bantam Books, 1972.

Goldstein, Joseph & Kornfield, Jack. *Seeking the Heart of Wisdom*. Boston: Shambala, 1986.

Goleman, Daniel. *The Varieties of the Meditative Experience*. New York: Dutton, 1977.

Hillman, James. *Insearch: Psychology and Religion*. New York: Charles Scribner's Sons, 1967.

Huxley, Aldous. *The Perennial Philosophy*. New York: Harper/Colophon Books, 1970.

Jacobi, Jolande. *The Way of Individuation*. New York: New American Library, 1967.

James, William. *The Varieties of Religious Experience*. New York: Collier, 1961.

Johnson, Robert A. *He: Understanding Masculine Psychology*. San Francisco: Harper & Row, 1974.

——. *She: Understanding Feminine Psychology*. San Francisco: Harper & Row, 1976.

Jung, Carl G. *Psychology and Religion*. New Haven, Conn.: Yale University Press, 1938.

——. *Memories, Dreams and Reflections*. New York: Pantheon Books, 1963.

——. Commentary in *The Secret of the Golden Flower: A Chinese Book of Life*, Translated by Richard Wilhelm. New York: Harvest Books, 1962.

——, ed. *Man and His Symbols*. New York: Dell, 1964.

Kornfield, Jack. *Living Buddhist Masters*. Santa Cruz, Calif.: Unity Press, 1977.

Kunkel, Fritz. *Creation Continues: A Psychological Interpretation of the Gospel of Matthew.* New York: Paulist Press, 1987.

Kurtz, Ernest. *AA: The Story.* San Francisco: Harper/Hazelden Books, 1988.

L., Elisabeth. *Twelve Steps for Overeaters.* San Francisco: Harper/Hazelden Books, 1988.

Levine, Stephen. *A Gradual Awakening.* New York: Anchor Press/Doubleday, 1979.

——. *Who Dies? An Investigation of Conscious Living and Conscious Dying.* New York: Anchor Press/Doubleday, 1982.

——. *Meetings at the Edge: Dialogues with the Grieving and the Dying, the Healing and the Healed.* New York: Anchor Press/Doubleday, 1984.

——. *Healing into Life and Death.* New York: Anchor Press/Doubleday, 1987.

Maslow, Abraham. *Toward a Psychology of Being.* Princeton, N.J.: Van Nostrand, 1962.

——. *Religion, Values and Peak Experiences.* New York: Viking Press, 1970.

——. *The Further Reaches of Human Nature.* New York: Viking Press, 1971.

May, Gerald G., M.D. *Addiction and Grace.* San Francisco: Harper & Row, 1988.

Merton, Thomas. *New Seeds of Contemplation.* New York: New Directions, 1962.

Needleman, Jacob. *The Heart of Philosophy.* New York: Bantam New Age Books, 1982.

Ornstein, Robert. *The Mind Field: A Personal Essay.* New York: Grossman, 1976.

Ram Dass. *The Only Dance There Is.* New York: Doubleday, 1974.

Ram Dass and Gorman, Paul. *How Can I Help.* New York: Alfred A. Knopf, 1985.

Ram Dass and Levine, Stephen. *Grist for the Mill.* Santa Cruz, Calif.: Unity Press, 1977.

Roth, Geneen. *Feeding the Hungry Heart: The Experience of Compulsive Eating.* New York: Signet, 1983.

——. *Breaking Free from Compulsive Overeating.* New York: Bobbs-Merrill, 1984.

Small, Jacquelyn. *Transformers: The Therapists of the Future.* Marina del Rey, Calif.: DeVorss, 1982.

Suzuki, Shunryu. *Zen Mind, Beginner's Mind.* New York: Walker/Weatherhill, 1970.

Tart, Charles, ed. *Transpersonal Psychologies.* New York: Harper & Row, 1977.

Tillich, Paul. *The Courage to Be.* New Haven, Conn.: Yale University Press, 1952.

Trungpa, Chogyam. *Cutting Through Spiritual Materialism.* Boulder, Colo.: Shambala Press, 1973.

Underhill, Evelyn. *Practical Mysticism.* Columbus, Ohio: Ariel Press, 1942.

Vaughn, Frances. *The Inward Arc: Healing & Wholeness in Psychotherapy & Spirituality.* Boston: New Science Library, 1986.

Weil, Andrew. *The Natural Mind: A New Way of Looking at Drugs and the Higher Consciousness.* New York: Houghton Mifflin, 1972.

Welwood, John, ed. *Awakening the Heart: East/West Approaches to Psychotherapy and the Healing Relationship.* Boulder, Colo.: New Science Library/Shambala, 1983.

Woods, Richard, ed. *Understanding Mysticism.* New York: Image Books/Doubleday, 1980.

Index

A

Abstinence, 24–25, 27–28, 116, 186–87. *See also* Pink cloud abstinence
Acceptance: of hardships, 112, 196; of self, 110, 127–28, 132
Addiction, cycle of, 146
Admission of powerlessness. *See* Powerlessness, admitting
Alcoholic insanity. *See* Sanity, restoration of
Alcoholics Anonymous, 29, 208; literature of, 60, 110, 194. *See also* Big Book (*Alcoholics Anonymous*); Twelve and Twelve
Alcoholism, 25–28, 36–41, 209–10
Alienation, 37–38, 64–65
Allergy theory, 22, 26–27, 186–87
Amends, making, 135–39, 141–42, 146–47, 153–67, 176. *See also* Living amends
Anger, 75–76, 175–77, 182–83, 218
Anxiety. *See* fear
Apologizing, 157–58
Archetypes, 61–62
Awareness. *See* Consciousness

B

Bare attention. *See* Consciousness

Bateson, Gregory, 37
Behavioral modification, 180
Bhagavad Gita, 195–96
Big Book (*Alcoholics Anonymous*), 36, 51–52, 92, 122, 146, 206; definition of alcoholism in, 26; on egocentricity, 59–60; first impressions of, 25; on human psyche, 58–59; on intuition, 198; on making amends, 156, 164; on *Promises of the Program*, 166–67; on recovery, 185–86; on relationships, 165; on self-condemnation, 175; on sharing moral inventory, 87–88; on spirituality, 34–35, 44–45
Bingeing, 6, 142–43, 172, 180–81, 182–83, 186–87, 189–90. *See also* Compulsive overeating
Blame, 43, 72–73, 78, 148
Bob, Dr. (early AA member), 34–35
Buber, Martin, 98
Buddhist tradition, 82–83, 128–32, 179–81, 191

C

Campbell, Joseph, 60–61
Character defects, 73, 79–85, 110–11, 115–16, 125; actions motivated by, 150–51,